한국어 몰라도 한국 여행 갈 수 있다!

KOREAN PHRASEBOOK
FOR TRAVELERS

written by Talk To Me In Korean

KOREAN PHRASEBOOK FOR TRAVELERS

한국어 몰라도 한국 여행 갈 수 있다!

1판 1쇄 • 1st Edition published	2016. 12. 25.	
2판 3쇄 • 3rd Edition published	2024. 7. 1.	

지은이 • Written by	Talk To Me In Korean
책임편집 • Edited by	선경화 Kyung-hwa Sun, 스테파니 베이츠 Stephanie Bates, 에밀리 프리즈러키 Emily Przylucki
디자인 • Designed by	선윤아 Yoona Sun
삽화 • Illustrations by	장성원 Sungwon Jang
녹음 • Voice Recordings by	김예지 Yeji Kim, 유승완 Seung-wan Yu
펴낸곳 • Published by	롱테일북스 Longtail Books
펴낸이 • Publisher	이수영 Su Young Lee
편집 • Copy-edited by	김보경 Florence Kim
주소 • Address	04033 서울특별시 마포구 양화로 113, 3층(서교동, 순흥빌딩)
	3rd Floor, 113 Yanghwa-ro, Mapo-gu, Seoul, KOREA
이메일 • E-mail	TTMIK@longtailbooks.co.kr
ISBN	979-11-86701-13-3 13710

*이 교재의 내용을 사전 허가 없이 전재하거나 복제할 경우 법적인 제재를 받게 됨을 알려 드립니다.

*잘못된 책은 구입하신 서점이나 본사에서 교환해 드립니다.

*Defective copies of this book may be exchanged at participating bookstores or directly from the publisher.

*The standard price of this book is printed on the back cover above the UPC barcode.

한국어 몰라도 한국 여행 갈 수 있다!

KOREAN PHRASEBOOK FOR TRAVELERS

written by Talk To Me In Korean

Introduction

When traveling to a foreign country with a different language, whether for business or vacation, it is not necessary to be fluent in that language or have perfect pronunciation. However, learning a few phrases in the local language, or carrying around a phrase book and knowing how to pronounce words as accurately as possible, does pay off and will greatly impress people with whom you are talking. Being able to communicate will make you feel more comfortable and at ease during your trip.

This book is designed for those traveling to Korea who find themselves wanting or needing to speak Korean without taking an expensive language course, having to download an expensive computer program, or download hundreds upon hundreds of audio files. Divided into sections by location and situation, Korean Phrasebook For Travelers covers nearly every situation which a traveler may encounter. Each word or phrase is written in Hangeul (the Korean written language) with a "romanization" (use of Roman characters to help with the pronunciation of Hangeul), and an English translation. The romanizations in this particular book have been modified from the "official romanization" system to better suit English speakers, and illustrations have been added to assist you in circumstances when communication has proven to be difficult.

Korean Phrasebook For Travelers is practical, informative, concise, and the perfect size to pack in your bag on your next trip to Korea.

Related phrases:

Sample phrases you may need to say or listen for in a certain situation.

Replaceable words:

The part(s) of speech that are marked with an <u>underline</u> mean you can replace it with a word that applies to your specific situation.

Other possibilities:

There are thousands of words that can be used as "replaceable words", but we have provided you with some of the most common words to use in a given situation. If you find you are having trouble being understood, simply show the illustration to a native speaker.

● **Related phrases:**

Where can I rent a car?
렌트카 어디서 빌려요?
Rehn-teu-kah aw-dee-saw beel-lyuh-yo?

Is there a <u>convenience store</u> near here?
이 주변에 <u>편의점</u> 있어요?
Ee joo-byuh-neh <u>pyuh-nee-jawm</u> ee-ssaw-yo?

● **Other possibilities:**

supermarket
대형 마트
deh-hyuhng mah-teu

grocery store
큰 슈퍼(마켓)
keun shyou-paw(-mah-keht)

corner shop
슈퍼(마켓)
shyou-paw(-mah-keht)

stream
계곡
gyeh-gok

sea
바다
bah-dah

Is this the train going towards Gangnam Station?
이거 강남역 가는 열차 맞아요?

No. It is heading in the opposite direction.
아니요. 반대 방향이에요

Ee-gaw **gahng-nahm-nyuhk** gah-neun yuhl-chah mah-jah-yo?

Ah-nee-yo. Bahn-deh bahng-hyahng-ee-eh-yo.

Sample dialogues:

Sample dialogues are often provided with an illustration of the situation.

Romanizations:

The romanizations in this particular book have been modified specifically for English speakers. They differ from the "official romanization" guide.

Related terms:
Words you may see or hear at a certain place are also provided with detailed illustrations.

Related terms:

Toner
스킨/토너
seu-keen/to-naw

Essence
에센스
eh-ssehn-seu

Moisturizer
수분크림
soo-boon-keu-reem

Track 06

Audio tracks :
This audio icon means that you can listen to native speakers' pronunciation for the words and phrases in the chapter, which are read for you in the direction of top to bottom and left to right. Listen to the audio tracks through our mobile app **TTMIK: Audio** or by downloading them at **https://talktomeinkorean.com/audio**.

Table of Contents

BASIC PHRASES

1. Greetings

Track 01

Hello.

안녕하세요.
Ahn-nyuhng-hah-seh-yo.

Goodbye.

안녕히 계세요. (When you are the person leaving and the other person stays)
Ahn-nyuhng-hee gyeh-seh-yo.

안녕히 가세요. (When the other person leaves and you stay, or when both of you leave at the same time)
Ahn-nyuhng-hee gah-seh-yo.

Thank you.

감사합니다.
Gahm-sah-hahm-nee-dah.

I am sorry.

죄송합니다.
Jweh-song-hahm-nee-dah.

2. Talking to a Stranger

Yes.

네.
Neh.

No.

아니요.
Ah-nee-yo.

Excuse me.

저기요. (when trying to get someone's attention)
Jaw-gee-yo.
잠시만요. (when moving/squeezing between people)
Jahm-shee-mahn-nyo.

Where am I? (on the map)
Where is it? (while pointing to a map)

여기가 어디예요?
Yuh-gee-gah aw-dee-yeh-yo?

Where is...?

...어디에 있어요?
···aw-dee-ay ee-ssaw-yo?

How can I get to...?

...어떻게 가요?
··· aw-ddaw-keh gah-yo?

3. Shopping

Do you have …?
Is there …?

…있어요?
…ee-ssaw-yo?

What is this?

이게 뭐예요?
Ee-geh mwo-yeh-yo?

How much is this?

이거 얼마예요?
Ee-gaw awl-mah-yeh-yo?

I will have this one.

이거 하나 주세요.
Ee-gaw hah-nah joo-seh-yo.

Is it free of charge?

무료예요?
Moo-ryo-yeh-yo?
공짜예요?
Gong-jja-yeh-yo?

What is this made of?

이거 뭘로 만들었어요?
Ee-gaw mwol-lo mahn-deu-raw-ssaw-yo?

4. Introducing yourself

What is your name?

이름이 뭐예요?
Ee-reu-mee mwo-yeh-yo?

My name is ...

제 이름은...이에요.
Jeh ee-reu-meun ... ee-eh-yo.

Where are you from?

어느 나라 사람이에요?
Aw-neu nah-rah sah-rah-mee-eh-yo?

I am from ...

저는...사람이에요.
Jaw-neun ⋯ sah-rah-mee-eh-yo.

USA
미국
mee-gook

Taiwan
대만
deh-mahn

Hong Kong
홍콩
hong-kong

Canada
캐나다
keh-nah-dah

China
중국
joong-gook

Philippines
필리핀
peel-lee-peen

UK
영국
yuhng-gook

Russia
러시아
raw-shee-ah

Singapore
싱가포르
seeng-gah-po-reu

France
프랑스
peu-rahng-sseu

Germany
독일
do-geel

Malaysia
말레이시아
mahl-lay-ee-shee-ah

Japan
일본
eel-bon

New Zealand
뉴질랜드
nyou-jeel-lehn-deu

Turkey
터키
taw-kee

Australia
호주
ho-joo

Cultural tip: When introducing yourself to a Korean person, you may be asked some very private questions, especially if that person is over 40 years old. They may ask your age, birth year, your blood type, or marital status, so if you are asked, try your best not to be offended or become defensive.

AT THE AIRPORT

You will probably encounter more people who speak English at the airport than at any other place in Korea. Should you need to speak to someone in Korean, the following are essential words and phrases to help you get to where you need to go.

Self check-in kiosk 무인 발권기
moo-een bahl-ggwon-gee

International boarding 국제선 탑승
gook-jjeh-sawn tahp-sseung

Check-in counter 체크인 카운터
cheh-keu-een kah-woon-taw

Pharmacy 약국
yahk-ggook

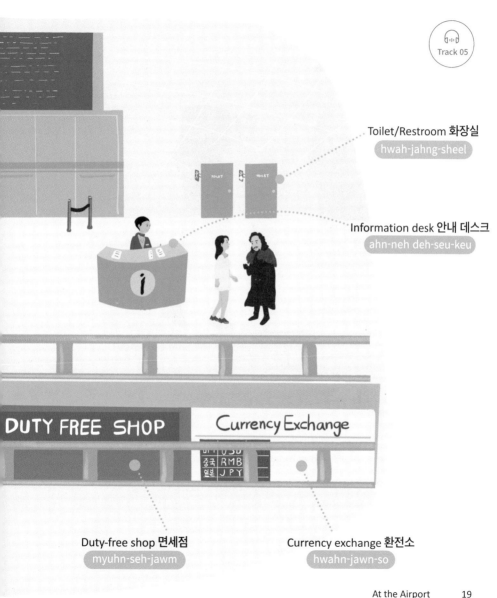

Toilet/Restroom 화장실
hwah-jahng-sheel

Information desk 안내 데스크
ahn-neh deh-seu-keu

DUTY FREE SHOP

Currency Exchange

Duty-free shop 면세점
myuhn-seh-jawm

Currency exchange 환전소
hwahn-jawn-so

1. Departures

Where can I exchange some currency?
환전 어디서 해요?

Please go to the 3rd floor.
3층으로 가시면 돼요.

Hwahn-jawn aw-dee-saw heh-yo?

Sahm-cheung-eu-ro gah-shee-myuhn dweh-yo.

Please refer to page 197
for building floor numbers.

Other possibilities:

Check-in
체크인
cheh-keu-een

Immigration
출국 심사
chool-gook sheem-sah

Transfer
환승
hwahn-seung

Phone charging station
휴대폰 충전
hyou-deh-pon choong-jawn

Related phrases:

Where can I buy souvenirs/duty-free goods?

기념품/면세품 어디서 살 수 있어요?

Gee-nyuhm-poom/myuhn-seh-poom aw-dee-saw sahl soo ee-saw-yo?

What is the gate number for this flight?

이 비행기는 몇 번 게이트에서 탑승해요?

Ee bee-hehng-gee-neun myuht bbawn gay-ee-teu-eh-saw tahp-sseung-heh-yo?

How long has it been delayed?

얼마나 지연됐어요?

Awl-mah-nah jee-yuhn-dweh-ssaw-yo?

The flight number I am taking is not on the screen.

제가 타는 비행기 편명이 전광판에 없어요.

Jeh-gah tah-neun bee-hehng-gee pyuhn-myuhng-ee jawn-gwahng-pah-neh awp-ssaw-yo.

2. Arrivals

Where are the restaurants?
식당 어디에 있어요?

They are over there.
저쪽에 있어요.

Sheek-ddahng aw-dee-ay ee-ssaw-yo?

Jaw-jjo-gay ee-saw-yo.

Other possibilities:

Café
카페
kah-peh

Convenience store
편의점
pyuh-nee-jawm

Bus stop
버스 정류장
baw-sseu jawng-ryou-jahng

Subway station
지하철역
jee-hah-chawl-lyuhk

Taxi stand
택시 정류장
tehk-shee jawng-nyou-jahng

Medical center
공항의료센터
gong-hahng-eu-ryo-ssehn-teo

Gate lounge for domestic flights
국내선 탑승동
goong-neh-sawn tahp-sseung-dong

Luggage storage facility
수하물 보관소
soo-hah-mool bo-gwahn-so

Tourist information center
관광 안내소
gwahn-gwahng ahn-neh-so

Smoking room
흡연실
heu-byuhn-sheel

Where can I take an express bus?
리무진 버스 어디서 타요?

You will see the bus stop if you go out gate 11.
11번 게이트로 나가시면 있어요.

Lee-moo-jeen baw-sseu aw-dee-saw tah-yo?

Shee-beel-bawn gay-ee-teu-ro nah-gah-shee-myuhn ee-ssaw-yo.

Other possibilities:

Taxi
택시
tehk-shee

Subway
지하철
jee-hah-chawl

Airport railroad express
공항철도
gong-hahang-chawl-ddo

Domestic flight
국내선
goong-neh-sawn

International flight
국제선
gook-jjeh-sawn

Bus bound for Gimpo Airport
김포 공항 가는 버스
geem-po gong-hahng gah-neun baw-sseu

Related phrases:

Where can I rent a car?

[렌터카] 어디서 빌려요?

Rehn-taw-kah aw-dee-saw beel-lyuh-yo?

Where can I pick up my luggage?

짐 어디서 찾아요?

Jeem aw-dee-saw chah-jah-yo?

Where can I buy a SIM card?

심카드 어디서 살 수 있어요?

Seem-kah-deu aw-dee-saw sahl soo ee-ssaw-yo?

My luggage isn't here yet.

제 짐이 아직 안 나왔어요.

Jeh jee-mee ah-jeek ahn nah-wah-ssaw-yo.

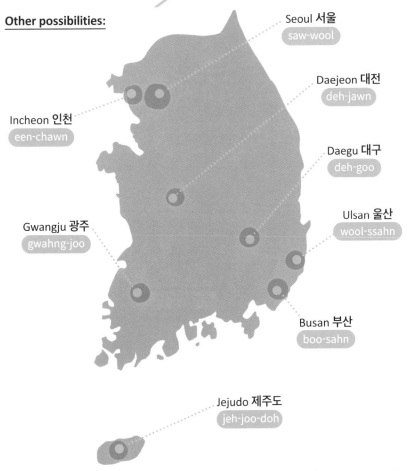

How can I go to <u>Daejeon</u> from here?

여기서 <u>대전</u> 어떻게 가요?

Yuh-gee-saw **deh-jawn** aw-ddaw-keh gah-yo?

<u>Other possibilities:</u>

Seoul 서울
saw-wool

Daejeon 대전
deh-jawn

Incheon 인천
een-chawn

Daegu 대구
deh-goo

Gwangju 광주
gwahng-joo

Ulsan 울산
wool-ssahn

Busan 부산
boo-sahn

Jejudo 제주도
jeh-joo-doh

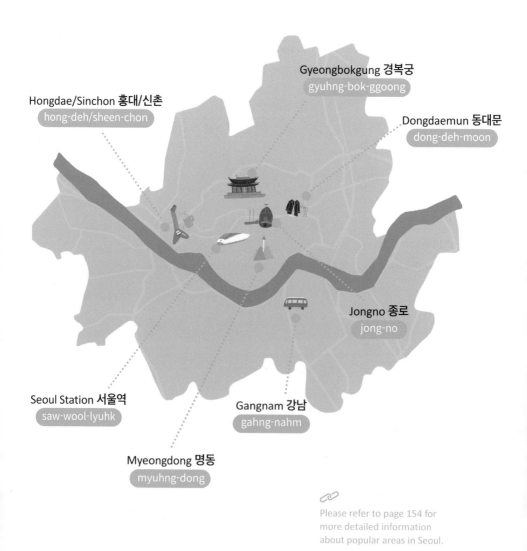

Gyeongbokgung 경복궁
gyuhng-bok-ggoong

Hongdae/Sinchon 홍대/신촌
hong-deh/sheen-chon

Dongdaemun 동대문
dong-deh-moon

Jongno 종로
jong-no

Seoul Station 서울역
saw-wool-lyuhk

Gangnam 강남
gahng-nahm

Myeongdong 명동
myuhng-dong

Please refer to page 154 for more detailed information about popular areas in Seoul.

GETTING AROUND

1. Taking the subway

Is this the train going towards Gangnam Station?
이거 강남역 가는 열차 맞아요?

No. It is heading in the opposite direction.
아니요. 반대 방향이에요.

Ee-gaw **gahng-nahm-nyuhk** gah-neun
yuhl-chah mah-jah-yo?

Ah-nee-yo. Bahn-deh bahng-hyahng-ee-eh-yo.

> **You should transfer at <u>Samgakji</u> Station to <u>line #6</u>.**
>
> <u>삼각지역</u>에서 <u>6호선</u>으로 갈아 타세요.
>
> <u>Sahm-gahk-jjee-yuh</u>-geh-saw **<u>you-ko-saw</u>**-neu-ro gah-rah tah-seh-yo.

<u>Other possibilities:</u>

Line 1	Line 2	Line 3	Line 4	Line 5
1호선	2호선	3호선	4호선	5호선
ee-ro-sawn	ee-ho-sawn	sah-mo-sawn	sah-ho-sawn	o-ho-sawn

Line 6	Line 7	Line 8	Line9
6호선	7호선	8호선	9호선
you-ko-sawn	chee-ro-sawn	pah-ro-sawn	goo-ho-sawn

Which exit do I need to go out of if I want to go to Ewha Womans University?
이화여대 가려면 몇 번 출구로 나가야 돼요?

You should go out exit 2 or 3.
2번이나 3번 출구로 나가시면 돼요.

Ee-hwah-yuh-deh gah-ryuh-myuhn myuht bbawn chool-goo-ro nah-gah-ya dweh-yo?

Ee-baw-nee-nah Sahm-bawn chool-goo-ro nah-gah-shee-myuhn dweh-yo.

Other possibilities:

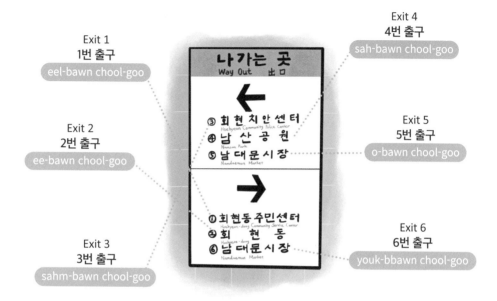

Exit 1
1번 출구
eel-bawn chool-goo

Exit 2
2번 출구
ee-bawn chool-goo

Exit 3
3번 출구
sahm-bawn chool-goo

Exit 4
4번 출구
sah-bawn chool-goo

Exit 5
5번 출구
o-bawn chool-goo

Exit 6
6번 출구
youk-bbawn chool-goo

Exit 7	Exit 8	Exit 9	Exit 10
7번 출구	8번 출구	9번 출구	10번 출구
cheel-bawn chool-goo	pahl-bawn chool-goo	goo-bawn chool-goo	sheep-bawn chool-goo
Exit 11	**Exit 12**	**Exit 13**	**Exit 14**
11번 출구	12번 출구	13번 출구	14번 출구
shee-beel-bawn chool-goo	shee-bee-bawn chool-goo	sheep-ssahm-bawn chool-goo	sheep-ssah-bawn chool-goo

2. Taking a bus

Track 09

Does this bus go to Rodeo Street in Apgujeong?
이 버스 압구정 로데오 거리 가요?

Yes. please get on.
네. 타세요.

Ee baw-sseu **ahp-ggoo-jawng ro-deh-o gaw-ree** gah-yo?

Neh. Tah-seh-yo.

Related phrases:

Is this Garosugil?

This place is Garosugil, right?

여기 가로수길 맞아요?

Yuh-gee **gah-ro-soo-ggeel** mah-jah-yo?

How much is the fare?

얼마예요?

Awl-mah-yeh-yo?

Let me get off!

내릴게요!

Neh-reel-ggeh-yo!

* If you transfer to another bus or subway, you need to swipe your transportation card when you get off the bus. Even if you don't transfer, it is safer to swipe your transportation card when you get off because some buses charge differently by distance.

Where should I take the bus to the War Memorial of Korea?

전쟁기념관 가는 버스 어디서 타요?

Jawn-jehng-gee-nyuhm-gwahn gah-neun baw-sseu aw-dee-saw tah-yo?

3. On the Street

Track 10

Excuse me, where is Namdaemun market?
저기요. 남대문 시장 어디 있어요?

You will find it if you go straight and turn left.
쭉 가시다가 왼쪽으로 가시면 돼요.

Jaw-gee-yo. **Nahm-deh-moon shee-jahng** aw-dee ee-ssaw-yo?

Jjook gah-shee-dah-gah wehn-jjo-geu-ro gah-shee-myuhn dweh-yo.

Related phrases:

Where are we (on the map)?

(Please let me know where we are on this map.)

지금 여기가 어디예요?

Jee-geum yuh-gee-gah aw-dee-yeh-yo?

Excuse me, could you please take a picture of us?

저기 죄송한데, 저희 사진 한 장만 찍어 주세요.

Jaw-gee jweh-song-hahn-deh, jaw-hee sah-jeen hahn jahng-mahn
jjee-gaw joo-seh-yo.

Related terms:

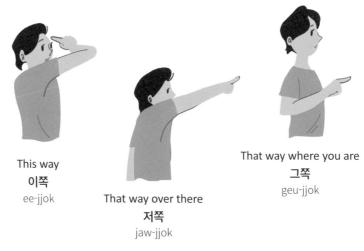

This way
이쪽
ee-jjok

That way over there
저쪽
jaw-jjok

That way where you are
그쪽
geu-jjok

Left
왼쪽
wehn-jjok

Right
오른쪽
o-reun-jjok

4. Taking a taxi

People who are not fluent in Korean often complain that it is difficult to communicate with taxi drivers in Korea. It is probably best to show the driver an exact address since all taxis have GPS. By using the "Kakao Taxi" application, you can submit a trip request in advance so the driver will already know your destination before you get in the car.

Related phrases:

BEFORE YOU GET IN A TAXI

Do you go to Myeongdong?

명동 가요?

Myuhng-dong gah-yo?

Sometimes you need to ask whether or not the driver will take you to your destination before you get in the car. When a driver lowers the window, you may ask this question.

WHEN YOU ARE IN A TAXI

Please take me to this place.

(while pointing out your destination on a map or showing the driver the address)

여기로 가 주세요.

Yuh-gee-ro gah joo-seh-yo.

Please take me to Hongik University Station.

홍대입구역 가 주세요.

Hong-day-eep-ggoo-yuhk gah joo-seh-yo.

Main gate of Hongik University, please.

홍대 정문이요.

Hong-deh jawng-moo-nee-yo.

It is next to Gangnam Post Office.

강남우체국 옆에 있어요.

Gahng-nah-moo-cheh-gook yuh-peh ee-ssaw-yo.

I will pay with a transportation card.

교통카드로 할게요.

Gyo-tong-kah-deu-ro hahl-ggeh-yo.

You can pay for a taxi ride with cash or a credit card. However as of December 2016, only Seoul taxis will additionally take transportation cards.

Please make a right here.

여기서 우회전이요.

Yuh-gee-saw **woo-hweh-jawn**-ee-yo.

Other possibilities:

Left turn
좌회전
jwah-hweh-jawn

Go straight
직진
jeek-jjeen

Right turn
우회전
woo-hweh-jawn

Do you want me to drop you off here?
여기서 세워 드릴까요?

Yes. Let me out here, please.
네. 여기서 세워 주세요.

Yuh-gee-saw seh-wo deu-reel-ggah-yo?

Neh. Yuh-gee-saw seh-wo joo-seh-yo.

ACCOMMODATIONS

1. At a hotel

Track 12

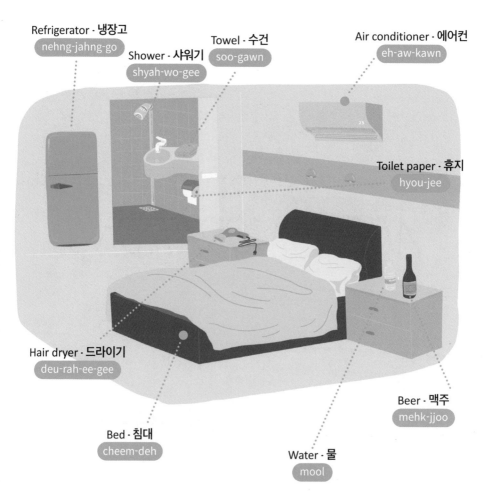

Refrigerator · 냉장고
nehng-jahng-go

Shower · 샤워기
shyah-wo-gee

Towel · 수건
soo-gawn

Air conditioner · 에어컨
eh-aw-kawn

Toilet paper · 휴지
hyou-jee

Hair dryer · 드라이기
deu-rah-ee-gee

Bed · 침대
cheem-deh

Water · 물
mool

Beer · 맥주
mehk-jjoo

Where do I have breakfast?
아침 식사는 어디서 해요?

Breakfast is available on the 2nd floor from 6 AM to 9 AM.
6시부터 9시까지고요. 2층으로 가시면 됩니다.

Ah-cheem sheek-ssah-neun aw-dee-saw heh-yo?

Yuh-sawt-shee-boo-taw **ah-hop-shee**-ggah-jee-go-yo.
Ee-cheung-eu-ro gah-shee-myuhn dwehm-nee-dah.

Please refer to page 194 for telling time, and page 197 for building floor numbers.

There is no <u>toilet paper</u> in my room. Would you please bring me some?

방에 <u>휴지</u> 없어요. 방으로 가져다 주세요.

Bahng-eh **hyou-jee** awp-ssaw-yo. bahng-eu-ro gah-jyuh-dah joo-seh-yo.

Other possibilities:

Toothbrush
칫솔
cheet-ssol

Toothpaste
치약
chee-yahk

Shampoo
샴푸
shyahm-poo

Soap
비누
bee-noo

Towel
수건
soo-gawn

Cup/Glass
컵
kawp

Wine glass
와인 잔
wah-een jahn

Fork
포크
po-keu

Knife
나이프
nah-ee-peu

Ice cubes
얼음
aw-reum

The shower is broken.

샤워기 고장 났어요.

Shyah-wo-gee go-jahng na-ssaw-yo.

Other possibilities:

Hair dryer
드라이기
deu-rah-ee-gee

TV
티비
tee-bee

Refrigerator
냉장고
nehng-jahng-go

Computer
컴퓨터
kawm-pyou-taw

Air conditioner
에어컨
eh-aw-kawn

Related phrases:

Please wake me up at <u>6 AM</u>.
아침 6시에 깨워 주세요.
Ah-cheem **yuh-sawt-shee**-eh ggeh-wo joo-seh-yo.

Is breakfast included?
아침 식사 포함이에요?
Ah-cheem sheek-ssah po-hah-mee-eh-yo?

I can smell cigarette smoke in my room.
방에서 담배 냄새 나요.
Bahng-eh-saw dahm-beh nehm-seh nah-yo.

I would like to change my room.
방 바꿔 주세요.
Bahng bah-ggwo joo-seh-yo.

The room is too small/hot/cold/noisy.

방이 너무 작아요/더워요/추워요/시끄러워요.

Bahng-ee naw-moo jah-gah-yo/daw-wo-yo/choo-wo-yo/shee-ggeu-raw-wo-yo.

Can I leave my bag here?

가방 맡길 수 있어요?

Gah-bahng maht-ggeel soo ee-ssaw-yo?

Could I borrow a multi adaptor/cell phone charger?

혹시 멀티 어댑터/핸드폰 충전기 빌릴 수 있을까요?

Hok-shee mawl-tee aw-dehp-taw/hehn-deu-pon choong-jawn-gee beel-leel soo ee-sseul-ggah-yo?

Could I extend my stay?

숙박 기간 연장할 수 있을까요?

Sook-bbahk gee-gahn yuhn-jahng-hahl soo ee-sseul-ggah-yo?

2. At a guesthouse

What time is check-out?
체크아웃 시간이 언제예요?

At 11 AM.
11시요.

Cheh-keu-ah-woot shee-gah-nee
awn-jeh-yeh-yo?

Yuh-rahn-shee-yo.

 Please refer to page 194 for telling time.

Related phrases:

I will be there around 5 o'clock to check in.

체크인 하러 5시쯤에 갈게요.

Cheh-keu-een hah-raw **dah-sawt-shee**-jjeu-meh gahl-ggeh-yo.

How can I get to the guest house from the airport?

공항에서 게스트하우스까지 어떻게 가요?

Gong-hahng-eh-saw geh-seu-teu-hah-woo-sseu-ggah-jee aw-ddaw-keh gah-yo?

Please refrain from going in and out/taking a shower after 11PM.

밤 11시 이후에는 출입을/샤워를 삼가 주세요.

Bahm yuh-rahn-shee ee-hoo-eh-neun **choo-ree-beul/shyah-wo-reul** sahm-gah joo-seh-yo.

Is there a convenience store near here?

이 주변에 편의점 있어요?

Ee joo-byuh-neh **pyuh-nee-jawm** ee-ssaw-yo?

Other possibilities:

supermarket
대형 마트

deh-hyuhng mah-teu

grocery store
큰 슈퍼(마켓)

keun shyou-paw(-mah-keht)

corner shop
슈퍼(마켓)

shyou-paw(-mah-keht)

stream
계곡

gyeh-gok

sea
바다

bah-dah

Are there any single rooms available from July 31st to August 2nd?
7월 31일부터 8월 2일까지 1인실 방 있어요?

Sorry. I am afraid not.
죄송합니다. 빈 방이 없습니다.

Chee-rwol sahm-shee-bee-reel-boo-taw **pah-rwol ee-eel**-ggah-jee **ee-reen-sheel** bahng ee-saw-yo?

Jweh-song-hahm-nee-dah. Been bahng-ee awp-sseum-nee-dah.

Other possibilities:

Two-person room
2인실
ee-een-sheel

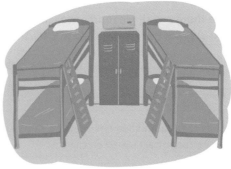

Dormitory
도미토리
do-mee-to-ree

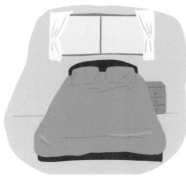

Double room
더블 침대 있는
daw-beul cheem-deh een-neun

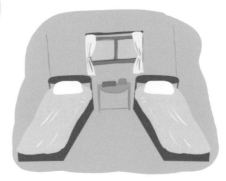

Twin room
싱글 침대 두 개 있는
sseeng-geul cheem-deh doo geh een-neun

If you need to book a room in Korea,
it is better to book your reservation
via text or email.

Please refer to page 192
for writing and pronouncing the date.

EATING

Related phrases:

Does this food have <u>meat</u> in it?

이 음식에 고기 들어가 있나요?

Ee eum-shee-geh **go-gee** deu-raw-gah een-nah-yo?

No <u>onions</u>, please.

양파 빼고 주세요.

<u>Yahng-pah</u> bbeh-go joo-seh-yo.

I am allergic to <u>nuts</u>.

견과류 알레르기가 있어요.

<u>Gyuhn-gwah-ryou</u> ahl-leh-reu-gee-gah ee-ssaw-yo.

I don't eat <u>pork</u>.

저는 <u>돼지고기</u> 안 먹어요.

Jaw-neun **dweh-jee-go-gee** ahn maw-gaw-yo.

Other possibilities:

Milk
우유
woo-you

Egg
계란
gyeh-rahn

Peanuts
땅콩
ddahng-kong

Flour
밀가루
meel-ggah-roo

Seafood
해산물
heh-sahn-mool

Fish
생선
sehng-sawn

Cucumber
오이
o-ee

Eggplant
가지
gah-jee

Peach
복숭아
bok-ssoong-ah

Apple
사과
sah-gwah

1. At a typical Korean restaurant

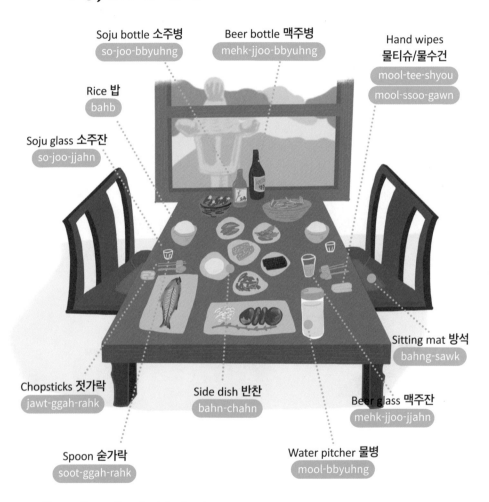

Soju bottle 소주병
so-joo-bbyuhng

Beer bottle 맥주병
mehk-jjoo-bbyuhng

Hand wipes
물티슈/물수건
mool-tee-shyou
mool-ssoo-gawn

Rice 밥
bahb

Soju glass 소주잔
so-joo-jjahn

Chopsticks 젓가락
jawt-ggah-rahk

Spoon 숟가락
soot-ggah-rahk

Side dish 반찬
bahn-chahn

Water pitcher 물병
mool-bbyuhng

Beer glass 맥주잔
mehk-jjoo-jjahn

Sitting mat 방석
bahng-sawk

How many are you?
몇 분이세요?

There are three of us.
세 명이요.

Myuht bboo-nee-seh-yo?

Seh myuhng-ee-yo.

If nobody asks how many are in your group,
you can generally just sit anywhere you want.

Other possibilities:

Counter for people: 명 myuhng

1 person
한 명
hahn myuhng

2 people
두 명
doo myuhng

3 people
세 명
seh myuhng

4 people
네 명
neh myuhng

5 people
다섯 명
dah-sawn myuhng

6 people
여섯 명
yuh-sawn myuhng

7 people
일곱 명
eel-gom myuhng

8 people
여덟 명
yuh-dawl myuhng

9 people
아홉 명
ah-hom myuhng

10 people
열 명
yuhl myuhng

Would you like to sit in a room?
방으로 가실래요?

No thanks. We are going to sit (at a table in the hall) here.
아니요. 여기 앉을게요.

Bahng-eu-ro gah-sheel-leh-yo?

Ah-nee-yo. Yuh-gee ahn-jeul-ggeh-yo.

Would you like to order?
주문하시겠어요?

One mul-naengmyeon and one bibim-naengmyeon, please.
물냉면 하나, 비빔냉면 하나 주세요.

Joo-moo-nah-shee-geh-ssaw-yo?

Mool-lehng-myuhn hah-nah, bee-beem-
nehng-myuhn hah-nah joo-seh-yo.

Other possibilities:

1 item
하나 / 한 개
hah-nah / hahn geh

2 items
두 개
doo geh

3 items
세 개
seh geh

4 items
네 개
neh geh

5 items
다섯 개
dah-sawt ggeh

6 items
여섯 개
yuh-sawt ggeh

7 items
일곱 개
eel-gop ggeh

8 items
여덟 개
yuh-dawl ggeh

9 items
아홉 개
ah-hop ggeh

10 items
열 개
yuhl ggeh

Typically, the counter "-개" is used with food served on individual plates, whereas "-인분" is used with food for multiple people served on a single plate or in a pot.

One serving
1인분
ee-reen-boon

Ten servings
10인분
shee-been-boon

Two servings	Three servings	Four servings
2인분	**3인분**	**4인분**
ee-een-boon	sah-meen-boon	sah-een-boon
Five servings	Six servings	Seven servings
5인분	**6인분**	**7인분**
o-een-boon	you-geen-boon	chee-reen-boon
Eight servings	Nine servings	
8인분	**9인분**	
pah-reen-boon	goo-een-boon	

Noodles

면 myuhn

Cold noodles in chilled broth
물냉면
mool-lehng-myuhn

Cold spicy mixed noodles
비빔냉면
bee-beem-nehng-myuhn

Cold buckwheat noodles
냉모밀
nehng-mo-meel

Hand torn noodle soup
수제비
soo-jeh-bee

Knife cut noodle soup
칼국수
kahl-gook-ssoo

Warm noodle soup/Feast noodles
잔치국수
jahn-chee-gook-ssoo

Spicy mixed noodles
비빔국수
bee-beem-gook-ssoo

Korean Stew

찌개 jjee-geh

After the Korean War ended, people who lived near the US Army base began making a stew from canned American food. 부대 means "army base", so this is how the stew got its name. Now it is a very popular dish!

Army base stew
부대찌개
boo-deh-jjee-geh

Kimchi stew
김치찌개
geem-chee-jjee-geh

Spicy soft tofu stew
순두부찌개
soon-doo-boo-jjee-geh

Soybean paste stew
된장찌개
dwehn-jahng-jjee-geh

Grilled Fish

생선 구이 sehng-sawn goo-ee

Grilled mackerel
고등어구이
go-deung-aw-goo-ee

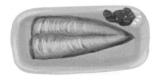

Grilled Japanese Spanish mackerel
삼치구이
sahm-chee-goo-ee

Grilled hairtail fish
갈치구이
gahl-chee-goo-ee

Pork Dishes

돼지고기 요리 dweh-jee-go-gee yo-ree

Spicy stir-fried pork
제육볶음
jeh-youk-bo-ggeum

Bulgogi hot pot stew
뚝배기불고기
ddook-bbeh-gee-bool-go-gee

Seasoned pork with rice
돼지불백
dweh-jee-bool-behk

Boiled pork wrap
보쌈
bo-ssahm

Seasoned & steamed pork feet
족발
jok-bbahl

Chicken Dishes

닭 요리 dahk yo-ree

Braised chicken with vegetables
찜닭
jjeem-dahk

Chicken soup with ginseng
삼계탕
sahm-gyeh-tahng

Spicy stir-fried chicken with vegetables
닭갈비
dahk-ggahl-bee

Plain/Spicy sauce fried chicken
후라이드/양념 치킨
hoo-rah-ee-deu/yahng-nyuhm chee-keen

Braised
Dishes

찜 요리 jjeem yo-ree

Braised assorted seafood
해물찜

heh-mool-jjeem

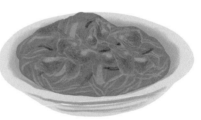

Braised monkfish
아귀찜

ah-gwee-jjeem

Braised short ribs
갈비찜

gahl-bee-jjeem

Bibimbap

비빔밥 bee-beem-bbahb

Mixed rice with assorted vegetables
야채비빔밥

(yah-cheh-bee-beem-bbahb)

Mixed rice with meat and assorted
vegetables in a hot stone bowl
돌솥비빔밥

(dol-sot-bee-beem-bbahb)

Mixed rice with beef tartare and
assorted vegetables
육회비빔밥

(you-khweh-bee-beem-bbahb)

Soup

탕 tahng

Spicy seafood soup
해물탕
[heh-mool-tahng]

> 탕 refers to seasoned meat, fish, and/or vegetables boiled in water to create a delicious soup.

Ox bone soup
곰탕
[gom-tahng]

Ox leg bone soup
설렁탕
[sawl-lawng-tahng]

Beef short ribs soup
갈비탕
[gahl-bee-tahng]

Pork bone and potato soup
감자탕
[gahm-jah-tahng]

2. At a Korean barbecue restaurant

Track 16

We will have two more servings of samgyeopsal please!

삼겹살 2인분 더 주세요!

Sam-gyuhp-ssahl ee-een-boon daw joo-seh-yo!

 Samgyeopsal is three layer pork belly.
It is high in fat and low in protein.

Other possibilities:

항정살 가브리살

등심

목살

안심

갈비 갈매기살

뒷다리살

앞다리살

삼겹살, 오겹살

Please refer to page 67
for counting food portions.

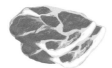

Pork neck · 목살
mok-ssahl

Fat and meat are well balanced.

Skirt steak · 갈매기살
gahl-meh-gee-ssahl

It is similar to thin skirt steak; tender and juicy.

Pork neck · 항정살
hahng-jawng-ssahl

Fat is spread out evenly, so it is tender

Pork cheek · 가브리살
gah-beu-ree-ssahl

A relatively lean, yet a very moist meat with a lot of connective tissue and collagen.

Ogyeopsal · 오겹살
o-gyuhp-ssahl

Five layer pork belly
(the same as samgyeopsal, just more layers!)

Water and side dishes are self-serve.

물이랑 반찬은 셀프입니다.

Moo-ree-rahng bahn-chah-neun sehl-peu-eem-nee-dah.

May I eat now?
이제 먹어도 돼요?

Yes. You may now eat.
네. 이제 드셔도 됩니다.

Ee-jeh maw-gaw-do dweh-yo?

Neh. Ee-jeh deu-shyuh-do dwehm-nee-dah.

In Korean restaurants, you often see food being cooked in a pot or on a grill at the table where you sit. A waiter/waitress will cook it for you, and when the food is ready to be eaten, he/she will let you know. If the restaurant is too busy and the waiter/waitress forgets to take care of your food, and you do not know what to do, just ask one of the waiters/waitresses if the food is ready by saying, "이제 먹어도 돼요?" [Ee-jeh maw-gaw-do dweh-yo?]

3. At a Korean fast food restaurant

Fritters

튀김 twee-geem

Squid fritters
오징어 튀김
o-jeeng-aw twee-geem

Spicy green pepper fritters
고추 튀김
go-choo twee-geem

Shrimp fritters
새우 튀김
seh-woo twee-geem

Vegetable fritters
야채 튀김
yah-cheh twee-geem

Sweet potato fritters
고구마 튀김
go-goo-mah twee-geem

Fishcake
오뎅/어묵
o-dehng/aw-mook

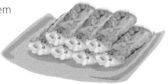

Sauteed glass noodles with vegetables
wrapped in seaweed and fried
김말이 튀김
geem-mah-ree twee-geem

Korean fast food

분식 boon-sheek

분식 originally means "flour-based food", but people nowadays think of 분식 as whatever you can find in a Korean fast food restaurant or a street vendor.

Spicy rice cakes
떡볶이
ddawk-bbo-ggee

Spicy rice cakes with instant noodles
라볶이
lah-bbo-ggee

Blood sausage
순대
soon-deh

Seaweed rice rolls
김밥 geem-bbahb

Cheese seaweed rice rolls
치즈 김밥
chee-jeu geem-bbahb

Tuna seaweed rice rolls
참치 김밥
chahm-chee geem-bbahb

라면 lah-myuhn

Instant noodles, the type that comes in a plastic package or a styrofoam cup, are commonly known as "ramen" in English. The English pronunciation of "ramen" [rah-mehn] is borrowed directly from the Japanese pronunciation, so please take special note of the Korean pronunciation of "ramen". If you say "ramen" as you would in English, native Korean speakers may think you want Japanese-style ramen. If you want Korean-style ramen, please remember to pronounce it as "lah-myuhn".

Cheese ramyeon
치즈 라면
chee-jeu lah-myuhn

Kimchi ramyeon
김치 라면
geem-chee lah-myuhn

Seafood ramyeon
해물 라면
heh-mool lah-myuhn

Rice cake ramyeon
떡 라면
ddawng lah-myuhn

4. At a food court

Do I order here?
주문 여기서 해요?

Yes. When the number on your ticket appears on the screen, please go get your food from the counter.
네. 여기서 하시고 번호표에 있는 번호가 전광판에 뜨면 가서 받으시면 돼요.

Joo-moon yuh-gee-saw heh-yo?

Neh. Yuh-gee-saw hah-shee-go baw-no-pyo-ay een-neun baw-no-gah jawn-gwahng-pah-neh ddeu-myuhn gah-saw bah-deu-shee-myuhn dweh-yo.

Related terms:

Menu
메뉴
meh-nyou

Order
주문
joo-moon

Receipt
영수증
yuhng-soo-jeung

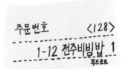

Number ticket
번호표
baw-no-pyo

Number display screen
전광판
jawn-gwahng-pahn

Return
반납
bahn-nahp

5. At a family restaurant

Is there anything else I can get you?
더 필요한 거 있으세요?

No. I'm ok.
아니요. 괜찮아요.

Daw pee-ryo-hahn gaw ee-sseu-seh-yo?

Ah-nee-yo. Gwehn-chah-nah-yo.

Related phrases:

Could I please have the menu back?
여기 메뉴판 좀 다시 주세요.
Yuh-gee meh-nyou-pahn jom dah-shee joo-seh-yo.

May I get a refill?
음료 리필 돼요?
Eum-lyo lee-peel dweh-yo?

In most Korean family restaurants, they only provide cola/Sprite as a refill even if you originally ordered a different drink.

Where do I pay?
계산 어디서 해요?
Gye-sahn aw-dee-saw heh-yo?

Please get me a refill with cola/Sprite.
콜라/스프라이트로 리필해 주세요.
Kol-lah/seu-peu-rah-ee-teu-ro lee-pee-reh joo-seh-yo.

Koreans hardly use the brand name when they order cola because restaurants usually have only Coca-Cola or Pepsi-Cola.

6. At a buffet

How much does it cost to eat lunch here?
여기 런치 얼마예요?

It is 20,000 won per person.
한 사람 당 2만 원이에요.

Yuh-gee lawn-chee awl-mah-yeh-yo?

Hahn sah-rahm dahng ee-mah nwo-nee-eh-yo.

7. At a bar/pub

What would you like to order?
뭐 드릴까요?

We will have two bottles of Chamisul soju, and one dish of spicy sea snails with noodles.
참이슬 두 병이랑 골뱅이 무침 하나 주세요.

Mwo deu-reel-ggah-yo?

Chah-mee-seul doo-byuhng-ee-rahng gol-behng-ee moo-cheem hah-nah joo-seh-yo.

Other possibilities:

 Alcoholic beverages

술 sool

Soju
소주
so-joo

Draft/Draught beer
생맥주
sehng-mehk-jjoo

Bottled beer
병맥주
byuhng-mehk-jjoo

Rice beer
막걸리
mahk-ggawl-lee

Bar snacks

안주 ahn-joo

literally translated as "snack which accompanies alcohol"

Dry snacks
마른 안주
mah-reun ahn-joo

Half-dried squid
반건조 오징어
bahn-gawn-jo o-jeeng-aw

Cuttlefish
한치
hahn-chee

Fruit-based snacks
과일 안주
gwah-eel ahn-joo

Fruit salad
과일 샐러드
gwah-eel sehl-law-deu

Fruit punch
과일 화채
gwah-eel hwah-cheh

Canned yellow peaches
황도
hwahng-do

Soup

탕 tahng

탕 refers to seasoned meat, fish, or vegetables boiled in water to create a delicious soup.

Mussel soup
홍합탕
hong-hahp-tahng

Fish cake soup
오뎅탕
o-dehng-tahng

Spicy fish roe soup
알탕
ahl-tahng

Spicy seafood soup
해물짬뽕탕
heh-mool-jjahm-bbong-tahng

Scorched rice soup
누룽지탕
noo-roong-jee-tahng

Grilled
철판
chawl-pahn

Stir-fried
볶음
bo-ggeum

Seasoned
무침
moo-cheem

Stir-fried kimchi with tofu
두부김치
doo-boo-geem-chee

Spicy chicken stew
닭볶음탕
dahk-bo-ggeum-tahng

Rolled omelette
계란말이
gye-rahn-mah-ree

Assorted sausages
모듬 소시지
mo-deum sso-shee-jee

Fried chicken
후라이드 치킨
hoo-rah-ee-deu chee-keen

Onion rings
어니언링
aw-nee-awn-leeng

French fries / Chips
감자 튀김
gahm-jah twee-geem

**Korean
pancake**

전 jawn

Green onion pancake
파전
pahh-jawn

Kimchi pancake
김치전
geem-chee-jawn

Chive pancake
부추전
boo-choo-jawn

8. At a cafe

Track 22

May I have an iced americano in a tall sized cup?
아이스 아메리카노 톨 사이즈로 한 잔 주세요.

Is a take-out cup okay?
테이크아웃 잔 괜찮으세요?

Ah-ee-seu ah-meh-ree-kah-no tol sah-ee-jeu-ro hahn jahn joo-seh-yo.

tay-ee-keu-ah-woot jahn gwehn-chah-neu-seh-yo?

Other possibilities:

Iced/hot
아이스/따뜻한
ah-ee-seu/ddah-ddeu-tahn

Americano
아메리카노
ah-meh-ree-kah-no

Cafe latte
카페라떼
kah-peh-lah-ddeh

Cappuccino
카푸치노
kah-poo-chee-no

Caramel macchiato
카라멜 마키아또
kah-rah-mehl mah-ggee-ah-ddo

Vanilla latte
바닐라 라떼
bah-neel-lah lah-ddeh

Short sized cup
숏 사이즈
shyot ssah-ee-jeu

Grande/large sized cup
그란데/라지 사이즈
geu-rahn-deh/lah-jee
ssah-ee-jeu

Tall/regular sized cup
톨/레귤러 사이즈
tol/leh-gyoul-law ssah-ee-jeu

Venti sized cup
벤티 사이즈
behn-tee ssah-ee-jeu

SHOPPING

Do you have this in a different color?

이거 다른 색깔 있어요?

Ee-gaw dah-reun sehk-ggahl ee-ssaw-yo?

Related terms:

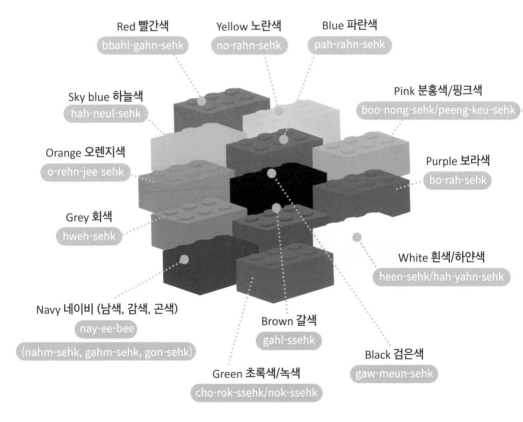

Red 빨간색
bbahl-gahn-sehk

Yellow 노란색
no-rahn-sehk

Blue 파란색
pah-rahn-sehk

Sky blue 하늘색
hah-neul-sehk

Pink 분홍색/핑크색
boo-nong-sehk/peeng-keu-sehk

Orange 오렌지색
o-rehn-jee-sehk

Purple 보라색
bo-rah-sehk

Grey 회색
hweh-sehk

White 흰색/하얀색
heen-sehk/hah-yahn-sehk

Navy 네이비 (남색, 감색, 곤색)
nay-ee-bee
(nahm-sehk, gahm-sehk, gon-sehk)

Brown 갈색
gahl-ssehk

Black 검은색
gaw-meun-sehk

Green 초록색/녹색
cho-rok-ssehk/nok-ssehk

Light
연한
yuh-nahn

Deep
진한
jee-nahn

Fluorescent
형광
hyuhng-gwahng

Bright
밝은
bahl-geun

Dark
어두운
aw-doo-woon

Pastel color/tone
파스텔 컬러/톤
pah-seu-tehl kawl-law/ton

Achromatic (greys, neutrals, blacks)
무채색
moo-cheh-sehk

Related phrases:

How much is this?
이거 얼마예요?
Ee-gaw awl-mah-yeh-yo?

Is this on sale?
이거 세일 상품이에요?
Ee-gaw say-eel sahng-poo-mee-eh-yo?

Related terms:

Discount
할인
hah-reen

Inventory
재고
jeh-go

Special offer products
기획 상품
gee-hwehk sahng-poom

Outlet store
상설 매장
sahng-sawl meh-jahng

Typically, if a store is a 상설 매장, it means that they carry clothes or accessories from past seasons at a discounted price.

1. At a clothing store

Fitting room 탈의실
tah-ree-sheel

Hanger 옷걸이
ot-ggaw-ree

Shop 매장
meh-jahng

Mirror 거울
gaw-wool

Warehouse/Storage 창고
chahng-go

Price tag 가격표/택
gah-gyuhk-pyo/tehk

Bar code 바코드
bah-ko-deu

Counter/Checkout 계산대
gyeh-sahn-deh

Display stand 매대
meh-deh

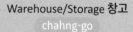

Do you have a bigger size?
더 큰 사이즈 있어요?

This is the only one left.
이거 하나 남았어요.

<u>Daw keun</u> ssah-ee-jeu ee-ssaw-yo?

Ee-gaw hah-nah na-ma-ssaw-yo.

Other possibilities:

smaller
더 작은
(daw jah-geun)

men's
남자
(nahm-jah)

women's
여자
(yuh-jah)

children's
아동용
(ah-dong-yong)

Women's tops

	XS 엑스스몰 ehk-sseu-seu-mol	S 스몰 seu-mol	M 미디움 mee-dee-woom	L 라지 lah-jee	XL 엑스라지 ehk-sseu-lah-jee
Korea	44 (85) 사사 (팔오) sah-sah (pah-ro)	55 (90) 오오 (구십) o-o (goo-sheep)	66 (95) 육육(구십오) young-nyouk (goo-shee-bo)	77 (100) 칠칠 (백) cheel-cheel (behk)	88 (105) 팔팔 (백오) pahl-pahl (beh-go)
USA	0-2	4-6	8-10	12-14	16-18
UK	4-6	8-10	10-12	16-18	20-22
Europe	34	36	38	40	42

Women's bottoms

Korea	26 이십육 ee-sheem-nyouk	28 이십팔 ee-sheep-pahl	30 삼십 sahm-sheep	32 삼십이 sahm-shee-bee	34 삼십사 sahm-sheep-ssah
USA	4	6	8	10	12
UK	8	10	12	14	16
Europe	36	38	40	42	44

You will often find some clothes in "free size" in Korea, especially tops, dresses, or leggings. "Free size" clothes are typically tailored for size 66 (95).

Men's tops

	S	M	L	XL	XXL
Korea	90 구십 goo-sheep	95 구십오 goo-shee-bo	100 백 behk	105 백오 beh-go	110 백십 behk-sheep
USA	14-14.5	14.5-15	15-15.5	15.5-16	16-16.5
UK	1	2	3	4	5
Europe	46	48	50	52	54

Men's bottoms

	28 이십팔 ee-sheep-pahl	30 삼십 sahm-sheep	32 삼십이 sahm-shee-bee	34 삼십사 sahm-sheep-ssah	36 삼십육 sahm-sheem-nyouk
Size (Korea)					
Waist (cm)	70	76	84	90	93

Men's wear in Korea is very "middle of the road" in terms of sizing. It is really difficult to find smaller or bigger sizes than what is listed above.

Unless you are buying clothes for someone else, it is HIGHLY recommended to try them on before purchasing.

Related phrases:

These clothes do not fit me.
옷이 안 맞아요.
o-shee ahn mah-jah-yo.

These clothes do not suit me.
옷이 저한테 안 어울려요.
o-shee jaw-hahn-teh ahn aw-wool-lyuh-yo.

These clothes are too big for me.
옷이 너무 커요.
o-shee naw-moo kaw-yo.

These clothes are too small for me.
옷이 너무 작아요.
o-shee naw-moo jah-gah-yo.

2. At a bag store

Natural leather
천연 가죽 chaw-nyuhn gah-jook

Ostrich	Crocodile	Snake
타조	악어	뱀
tah-jo	ah-gaw	behm

Cow	Goat	Eel
소	염소	장어
so	yuhm-so	jahng-aw

Calf	Buffalo	Lizard
송아지	버팔로	도마뱀
song-ah-jee	baw-pahl-lo	do-mah-behm

Sheep
양
yahng

Artificial/Synthetic leather
인조 가죽/합성 피혁
een-jo gah-jook/hahp-ssawng pee-hyuhk

Related phrases:

Is this genuine leather?
이거 가죽이에요?
Ee-gaw gah-joo-gee-eh-yo?

Which country is this brand from?
어느 나라 브랜드예요?
Aw-neu nah-rah beu-rehn-deu-yeh-yo?

Is this a(n) Korean brand?
이거 <u>한국</u> 브랜드예요?
Ee-gaw **hahn-gook** beu-rehn-deu-yeh-yo?

Please refer to page 15 for country names.

You may try it on.
한번 메 보세요.
Hahn-bawn meh bo-seh-yo.

3. At an accessory/jewelry store

Is this 14K gold?
이거 14K예요?

No. It is gold plated.
아니요. 도금이에요.

Ee-gaw sheep-ssah-kay-ee-yeh-yo?

Ah-nee-yo. Do-geu-mee-eh-yo.

Related terms:

Earrings
귀걸이/귀고리
gwee-gaw-ree/gwee-go-ree

Bracelet
팔찌
pahl-jjee

Necklace
목걸이
mok-ggaw-ree

Ring
반지
bahn-jee

Brooch
브로치
beu-ro-chee

Hairclip
머리핀
maw-ree-peen

Ponytail holder
머리끈
maw-ree-ggeun

14K gold
14K
sheep-ssah-kay-ee

14K gold = 58.3% gold

18K gold
18K
sheep-pahl-kay-ee

18K gold = 75% gold

24K gold
24K
ee-sheep-sah-kay-ee

24K gold = 99.99% gold

Gold
금
geum

Silver
은
eun

Rose gold
로즈골드
ro-jeu-gol-deu

White gold
화이트골드
hwah-ee-teu-gol-deu

Pendant
펜던트
pehn-dawn-teu

Chain
줄
jool

Cubic zirconia
큐빅
kyou-beek

Related phrases:

The chain is too long.
줄이 길어요.
Joo-ree gee-raw-yo.

The chain is too short.
줄이 짧아요.
Joo-ree jjahl-bah-yo.

The ring is too big.
반지가 커요.
Bahn-jee-gah kaw-yo.

The ring is too small.
반지가 작아요.
Bahn-jee-gah jah-gah-yo.

4. At a Shoe Store

> **Do you have these shoes in size 230?**
> 이 신발 230 사이즈 있어요?

> **Wait a minute. I will check.**
> 네. 잠시만 기다리세요. 확인해 볼게요.

> Ee sheen-bahl **ee-behk-sahm-sheep** ssah-ee-jeu ee-ssaw-yo?

> Ne. Jahm-shee-mahn gee-dah-ree-seh-yo. Hwah-gee-neh bol-ggeh-yo.

Size chart

Women			
Korea	USA	UK	Europe
220 · 이백이십 ee-beh-gee-sheep	5	3	36
225 · 이백이십오 ee-beh-gee-shee-bo	5.5	3.5	36.5
230 · 이백삼십 ee-behk-sahm-sheep	6	4	37
235 · 이백삼십오 ee-behk-sahm-shee-bo	6.5	4.5	37.5
240 · 이백사십 ee-behk-sah-sheep	7	5	38
245 · 이백사십오 ee-behk-sa-shee-bo	7.5	5.5	38.5
250 · 이백오십 ee-beh-go-sheep	8	6	39
255 · 이백오십오 ee-beh-go-shee-bo	8.5	6.5	39.5
260 · 이백육십 ee-behng-nyouk-sheep	9	7	40
265 · 이백육십오 ee-behng-nyouk-shee-bo	9.5	7.5	40.5
270 · 이백칠십 ee-behk-cheel-sheep	10	8	41

Men			
Korea	USA	UK	Europe
245 · 이백사십오 ee-behk-sah-shee-bo	6.5	5.5	40
250 · 이백오십 ee-beh-go-sheep	7	6	40.5
255 · 이백오십오 ee-beh-go-shee-bo	7.5	6.5	41
260 · 이백육십 ee-behng-nyouk-sheep	8	7	41.5
265 · 이백육십오 ee-behng-nyouk-shee-bo	8.5	7.5	42
270 · 이백칠십 ee-behk-cheel-sheep	9	8	42.5
275 · 이백칠십오 ee-behk-cheel-shee-bo	9.5	8.5	43
280 · 이백팔십 ee-behk-pahl-sheep	10	9	43.5
285 · 이백팔십오 ee-behk-pahl-shee-bo	10.5	9.5	44
290 · 이백구십 ee-behk-goo-sheep	11	10	44.5
295 · 이백구십오 ee-behk-goo-shee-bo	11.5	10.5	45

Related terms:

Sneakers/Trainers
운동화
woon-dong-hwah

Loafers
로퍼
lo-paw

Sandals
샌들
ssehn-deul

Slippers
슬리퍼
seul-lee-paw

Low heel shoes
단화
dah-nwah

High heels
하이힐
hah-ee-heel

Wedge heels
웨지힐
weh-jee-heel

Peep/Open toe
오픈토
o-peun-to

Flat shoes
플랫슈즈
peul-leht-shyou-jeu

Platform heel
가보시힐
gah-bo-shee-heel

Shoelaces
신발 끈
sheen-bahl ggeun

Shoelaces for sneakers
운동화 끈
woon-dong-hwah ggeun

Shoelaces for dress shoes
구두 끈
goo-doo ggeun

Related phrases:

The heels are too high.

굽이 너무 높아요.

Goo-bee naw-moo no-pah-yo.

The heels are too low.

굽이 너무 낮아요.

Goo-bee naw-moo nah-jah-yo.

The heels are too thin.

굽이 너무 가늘어요.

Goo-bee naw-moo gah-neu-raw-yo.

The heels are too thick.

굽이 너무 굵어요.

Goo-bee naw-moo gool-gaw-yo.

Heel

굽

goop

Shoehorn

구둣주걱

goo-doot-jjoo-gawk

5. At a cosmetics store

Who is this item for?
누가 쓰실 거예요?

I will give this to my mom as a present.
엄마한테 선물할 거예요.

Noo-gah sseu-sheel ggaw-yeh-yo?

Awm-mah-hahn-teh sawn-moo-rahl ggaw-
yeh-yo.

Other possibilities:

Friend
친구
cheen-goo

Dad
아빠
ah-bbah

Younger sister/brother
동생
dong-sehng

Older sister
(from a female's perspective)
언니
awn-nee

Older sister
(from a male's perspective)
누나
noo-nah

Girlfriend
여자 친구
yuh-jah cheen-goo

Boyfriend
남자 친구
nahm-jah cheen-goo

Older brother
(from a male's perspective)
형
hyuhng

Older brother
(from a female's perspective)
오빠
o-bbah

Related terms:

Toner
스킨/토너
seu-keen/to-naw

Essence
에센스
eh-ssehn-seu

Moisturizer
수분크림
soo-boon-keu-reem

Serum
세럼
sseh-rawm

Sunscreen
선크림
ssawn-keu-reem

Eye cream
아이크림
ah-ee-keu-reem

Foundation
파운데이션
pah-woon-day-ee-shyuhn

Makeup base
메이크업 베이스
may-ee-keu-awp bay-ee-seu

Primer
프라이머
peu-rah-ee-maw

Concealer
컨실러
kawn-seel-law

Eyeliner
아이라이너
ah-ee-lah-ee-naw

Mascara
마스카라
mah-seu-kah-rah

Eye shadow
아이섀도
ah-ee-shyeh-do

Eyebrow pencil
아이브로펜슬
ah-ee-beu-ro-pehn-seul

Brush
브러시
beu-raw-shee

Lip gloss
립글로즈
leep-geul-lo-jeu

Blusher
블러셔
beul-law-shyuh

Lipstick
립스틱
leep-sseu-teek

Lip balm
립밤
leep-bbahm

Oily skin
지성 피부
jee-sawng pee-boo

Dry skin
건성 피부
gawn-sawng pee-boo

Combination skin
복합성 피부
bo-kahp-ssawng pee-boo

Acne
여드름
yuh-deu-reum

Freckles
기미
gee-mee

Wrinkles
주름
joo-reum

Pigmentation
색소 침착
sehk-so cheem-chahk

Anti-aging
항노화/안티에이징
hahng-no-hwah/ahn-tee-eh-ee-jeeng

Whitening
미백/화이트닝
mee-behk/hwah-ee-teu-neeng

Moisturizing
보습
bo-seup

Sun protection
자외선 차단
jah-weh-sawn chah-dahn

Soothing
진정
jeen-jawng

Wrinkle treatment
주름 개선
joo-reum geh-sawn

Elasticity
탄력
tahl-lyuhk

Skin regeneration
피부 재생
pee-boo jeh-sehng

6. At a convenience store

Feminine products
여성용품
yuh-sawng-yong-poom

Stockings/Tights/Pantyhose
스타킹
seu-tah-keeng

Instant noodles in a styrofoam cup
컵라면
kawm-lah-myuhn

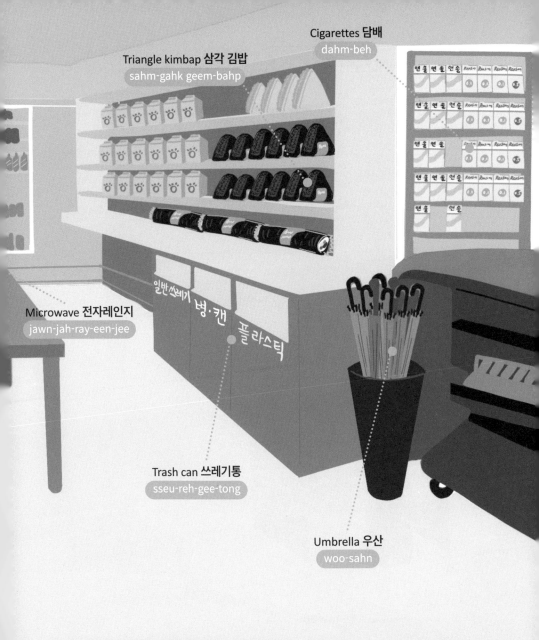

Cigarettes 담배
dahm-beh

Triangle kimbap 삼각 김밥
sahm-gahk geem-bahp

Microwave 전자레인지
jawn-jah-ray-een-jee

일반쓰레기 병·캔 플라스틱

Trash can 쓰레기통
sseu-reh-gee-tong

Umbrella 우산
woo-sahn

Do you have hand wipes?
물티슈 있어요?

Yes. They are at the end of that row.
네. 저쪽 끝으로 가 보세요.

Mool-tee-shyou ee-ssaw-yo?

Ne. Jaw-jjok ggeu-teu-ro gah bo-seh-yo.

Other possibilities:

Tissue
휴지
(hyou-jee)

Painkillers/Analgesic
진통제
(jeen-tong-jeh)

Fever-reducing medicine
해열제
(heh-yuhl-jjeh)

Transportation card
교통카드
(gyo-tong-kah-deu)

Toiletries
세면도구
(seh-myuhn-do-goo)

Charger
충전기
(choong-jawn-gee)

Razor
면도기
(myuhn-do-gee)

Pre-packed meal
도시락
(do-shee-rahk)

Pen
펜
(pehn)

Notepad
메모지
(meh-mo-jee)

Batteries
건전지
(gawn-jawn-jee)

Sanitary napkins
생리대
(sehng-lee-deh)

Tampons
탐폰
(tahm-pon)

7. At a big supermarket

Where is the cereal?
시리얼 어디에 있어요?

They are in the snacks section over there.
저쪽 과자 코너에 있어요.

Ssee-ree-awl aw-dee-eh ee-ssaw-yo?

Jaw-jjok gwah-jah ko-naw-eh ee-ssaw-yo.

Other possibilities:

Toothbrush
칫솔
cheet-ssol

Toothpaste
치약
chee-yahk

Laver/Dried roasted seaweed
김
geem

Alcohol
술
sool

Soju
소주
so-joo

Beer
맥주
mehk-jjoo

Wine
와인
wah-een

Paper cups
종이컵
jong-ee-kawp

Cosmetics
화장품
hwah-jahng-poom

Clothes
옷
ot

Underwear
속옷
so-got

8. At a traditional market

How much is this?
이거 얼마예요?

It is 3,000 won.
3천원.

Ee-gaw awl-mah-yeh-yo?

Sahm-chaw-nwon.

Related phrases:

What is this?
이거 뭐예요**?**

Ee-gaw mwo-yeh-yo?

It is too expensive.
너무 비싸요**.**

Naw-moo bee-ssah-yo.

Please give me a discount.
싸게 주세요**.**

Ssah-geh joo-seh-yo.

Is it good/tasty?
이거 맛있어요**?**

Ee-gaw mah-shee-saw-yo?

It is so good/tasty.
너무 맛있어요**.**

Naw-moo mah-shee-saw-yo.

Please give me a lot.
많이 주세요**.**

Mah-nee joo-seh-yo.

Cultural tip: Traditional markets are the only places where you can haggle.

FUN PLACES

1. At a palace

During the Joseon Dynasty, "Five Grand Palaces" were built in Seoul – Changdeokgung, Changgyeonggung, Deoksugung, Gyeongbokgung, and Gyeonghuigung – all of which are located in the Jung District (중구 [joong-goo]) and Jongno District (종로구 [jong-no-goo]).

Changgyeong Palace
창경궁 chahng-gyuhng-goong

Originally the Summer Palace of the Goryeo King, it later became one of the Five Grand Palaces of the Joseon Dynasty.

Gyeongbok Palace
경복궁 gyuhng-bok-ggoong

This was the main royal palace of the Joseon Dynasty, and is now the most famous palace in Korea.

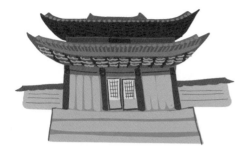

Changdeok Palace
창덕궁 chahng-dawk-ggoong

This palace was built in 1395 to be used as the primary palace when Gyeongbok Palace was unable to be used for any reason, such as during a war.

Deoksu Palace
덕수궁 dawk-ssoo-goong

This residence became a royal 'palace' during the Imjin War in 1592 after all of the other palaces had burned down.

Gyeonghui Palace

경희궁 gyuhng-hee-goong

During the late Joseon period, this palace served as an emergency residence for the king.

Related phrases:

Where is the entrance?

입구가 어디예요?

Eep-ggoo-gah aw-dee-yeh-yo?

Where is the exit?

출구가 어디예요?

Chool-goo-gah aw-dee-yeh-yo?

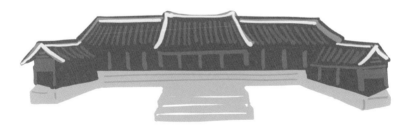

Jongmyo Shrine

종묘 jong-myo

A Confucian shrine dedicated to the perpetuation of memorial services for the deceased kings and queens of the Korean Joseon Dynasty.

2. On a mountain

Related phrases:

How much further until I get to the top?
정상까지 얼마나 남았어요?
Jawng-sahng-ggah-jee awl-mah-nah nah-mah-ssaw-yo?

Where do I take the cable car?
케이블카 어디서 타요?
Kay-ee-beul-kah aw-dee-saw tah-yo?

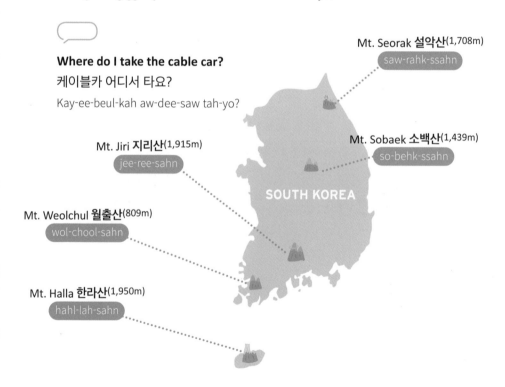

Mt. Seorak 설악산(1,708m)
saw-rahk-ssahn

Mt. Sobaek 소백산(1,439m)
so-behk-ssahn

Mt. Jiri 지리산(1,915m)
jee-ree-sahn

SOUTH KOREA

Mt. Weolchul 월출산(809m)
wol-chool-sahn

Mt. Halla 한라산(1,950m)
hahl-lah-sahn

Mt. Dobong 도봉산(740m)
do-bong-sahn

Mt. Bukhan 북한산(837m)
boo-kahn-sahn

Mt. Inwang 인왕산(338m)
ee-nwahng-sahn

Mt. Bugak 북악산(342m)
boo-gahk-ssahn

Mt. Nam 남산(262m)
nahm-sahn

SEOUL

Mt. Cheonggye 청계산(618m)
chawng-gyeh-sahn

Mt. Gwanak 관악산(629m)
gwah-nahk-ssahn

Even if you have never been hiking, it is definitely worth giving it a go while you are in Korea. There are so many mountains in Korea, ranging from very short and easy hikes to all day hikes with a number of trails of varying difficulty, that only a handful could be labeled on this map. If you are a novice hiker, we recommend starting with a few of the shorter mountains before tackling the taller ones.

Excuse me. I hurt my leg. Please help me.

저기요. 다리를 다쳤어요. 좀 도와주세요.

Jaw-gee-yo. **Dah-ree**-reul dah-chyuh-ssaw-yo. Jom do-wah-joo-seh-yo.

Other possibilities:

Head 머리
maw-ree

Arm 팔
pahl

Bottom/Rear end 엉덩이
awng-dawng-ee

Wrist 손목
son-mohk

Hand 손
son

Thigh 허벅지
haw-bawk-jjee

Knee 무릎
moo-reup

Calf 종아리
jong-ah-ree

Toe 발가락
bahl-ggah-rahk

Ankle 발목
bahl-mok

Please refer to page 178
for more body part terms.

3. At a theme park

What time do you open/close?
개장/폐장 시간이 언제예요?

At 11.
11시예요

Geh-jahng/Pyeh-jahng shee-gah-nee awn-jeh-yeh-yo?

Yuh-rahn-shee-yeh-yo.

Related terms:

Admission ticket
입장권
(eep-jjahng-ggwon)

Daytime ticket
주간권
(joo-gahn-ggwon)

Nighttime ticket
야간권
(yah-gahn-ggwon)

All-inclusive pass
자유 이용권
(jah-you ee-yong-ggwon)

Waiting line
대기 라인
(deh-gee lah-een)

Related phrases:

How long do I have to wait?
얼마나 기다려야 돼요?
Awl-mah-nah gee-dah-ryuh-yah dweh-yo?

When does the parade start?
퍼레이드 언제 시작해요?
Paw-ray-ee-deu awn-jeh shee-jah-keh-yo?

Where is the restroom?
화장실 어디 있어요?
Hwah-jahng-sheel aw-dee ee-ssaw-yo?

Where can I see the performance?
공연 어디서 해요?
Gong-yuhn aw-dee-saw heh-yo?

Is this the line for Thunder Falls?

이 줄이 <u>썬더폴스</u> 줄 맞아요?

Ee joo-ree **ssawn-daw-pol-sseu** jool mah-jah-yo?

 Generally, each ride in a Korean amusement park has its own park-specific name. For example, "T-Express" and "Rolling X-Train" are two rollercoasters at Everland. However, the following four types of rides are almost always referred to as their general name rather than their park-specific name.

Other possibilities:

Carousel
회전목마
hweh-jawn-mong-mah

Viking boat
바이킹
bah-ee-keeng

Ferris wheel
관람차
gwahl-lahm-chah

Bumper cars
범퍼카
bawm-paw-kah

4. At a water park

Where can I rent a life jacket?
구명조끼 어디서 빌릴 수 있어요?
Goo-myuhng-jo-ggee aw-dee-saw beel-leel ssoo ee-ssaw-yo?

Other possibilities:

Swimsuit
수영복
soo-yuhng-bok

Beach chair
비치 체어
bee-chee cheh-aw

Towel
타월
tah-wol

Related phrases:

Can I go out and come back in?

잠깐 나갔다 와도 돼요?

Jahm-ggahn nah-gaht-ddah wah-do dweh-yo?

Where can I buy this/that?

이건/저건 어디서 팔아요?

Ee-gawn/jaw-gawn aw-dee-saw pah-rah-yo?

If you are pointing at something close to you, you say 이건[ee-gawn], and if you are pointing at something far from you, you say 저건[jaw-gawn].

Where can I take the bus to Seoul?

서울 가는 버스 어디서 타요?

Saw-wool gah-neun baw-sseu aw-dee-saw tah-yo?

Do I have to pay for this?

이거 돈 내고 쓰는 거예요?

Ee-gaw don neh-go sseu-neun gaw-yeh-yo?

Morning ticket 오전권 o-jawn-ggwon	Adult 대인 day-een	22,000
	Child 소인 so-een	16,000
	Senior citizen 경로 gyuhng-no	16,000
Afternoon ticket 오후권 o-hoo-ggwon	Adult 대인 day-een	22,000
	Child 소인 so-een	16,000
	Senior citizen 경로 gyuhng-no	16,000
1-day ticket 1일권 ee-reel-ggwon	Adult 대인 day-een	40,000
	Child 소인 so-een	29,000
	Senior citizen 경로 gyuhng-no	29,000
2-day ticket 2일권 ee-eel-ggwon	Adult 대인 day-een	60,000
	Child 소인 so-een	43,000
	Senior citizen 경로 gyuhng-no	43,000

Related terms:

Phone charging
휴대폰 충전
hyou-deh-pon choong-jawn

Valuables storage
귀중품 보관
gwee-joong-poom bo-gwahn

Locker
락커
lahk-kaw

Operating hours
운영 시간
woo-nyuhng shee-gahn

Balance refund
잔액 환불
jah-nehk hwahn-bool

Re-entry
재입장
jay-eep-jjahng

Belongings inspection
소지품 검사
so-jee-poom gawm-sah

Shower room
샤워실
shyah-wo-sheel

5. At a Ski resort

Related terms:

Lift ticket
리프트권
lee-peu-teu-ggwon

Helmet
헬멧
hehl-meht

Equipment rental
장비 렌탈
jahng-bee rehn-tahl

Snowboard
스노보드
seu-no-bo-deu

Ski
스키
seu-kee

Goggles
고글
go-geul

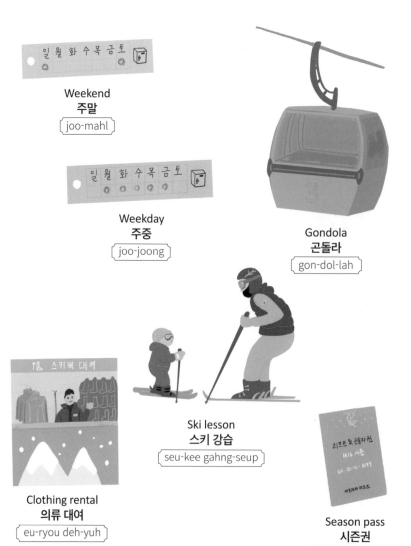

Weekend
주말
[joo-mahl]

Weekday
주중
[joo-joong]

Gondola
곤돌라
[gon-dol-lah]

Ski lesson
스키 강습
[seu-kee gahng-seup]

Clothing rental
의류 대여
[eu-ryou deh-yuh]

Season pass
시즌권
[ssee-jeun-ggwon]

FESTIVALS IN KOREA

The exact date and place where festivals are held varies every year.
Be sure to research the details before you make plans.

Track 37

 Spring flower festivals
봄꽃 축제 bom-ggot chook-jjeh

Yeongdeungpo Yeouido Spring Flower Festival
영등포 여의도 봄꽃 축제 yuhng-deung-po yuh-ee-do bom-ggot chook-jjeh

The most famous cherry blossom festival in Seoul. (Mid April)

Jinhae Gunhangje Festival
진해 군항제 jee-neh goo-nahng-jeh

The biggest cherry blossom festival in Korea. (Mid April)

Jeju Rapeseed Festival

제주 유채꽃 큰 잔치 jeh-joo you-cheh-ggot keun jahn-chee

The most famous and popular festival on Jeju Island. (Mid April)

Everland Tulip Festival / Rose Festival

에버랜드 튤립 축제/장미 축제
eh-baw-rehn-deu tyoul-leep chook-jje/jahng-mee chook-jjeh

Unlike cherry blossoms or rapeseed flowers which you can see in many places throughout Korea, it is really difficult to find as many tulips and roses anywhere else in the country as are at this festival. In order to attend this festival, you must buy a ticket to Everland! (Late March ~ Mid June)

 ### Beach festivals
바다 축제 bah-dah chook-jjeh

Boryeong Mud Festival

보령 머드 축제 bo-ryuhng maw-deu chook-jjeh

One of the most popular festivals among foreigners in Korea, the mud festival is just what it sounds like: a festival celebrating mud! To be more specific, this festival celebrates the cosmetic and beneficial properties of the mud from the area of Daecheon. There are many attractions including mud massage, mud wrestling, zipline, inflatables, mud skiing, and even a mud fireworks fantasy!

Busan Sea Festival

부산 바다 축제 boo-sahn bah-dah chook-jjeh

For about one week, there are many events and festivals on several beaches in Busan combined under one name. Such events include a water sports contest, dance festival, and various music concerts. (Early August)

Firework festivals
불꽃 축제 bool-ggot chook-jjeh

Seoul International Fireworks Festival

서울 세계 불꽃 축제 saw-wool seh-gyeh bool-ggot chook-jjeh

The most famous fireworks festival in Korea. You can expect to see nearly the whole city in attendance. (Early October)

Pohang International Fireworks Festival

포항 국제 불빛 축제 po-hahng gook-jjeh bool-bbeet chook-jje

You can enjoy the sea, night market, and sights of Pohang as well as the fireworks. (Late July ~ Early August)

Winter festivals
겨울 축제 gyuh-wool chook-jjeh

Homigot Sunrise Festival
호미곶 한민족 해맞이 축전
ho-mee-got hahn-meen-jok heh-mah-jee chook-jjawn

Homigot is the place where the sun rises the earliest in Korea. You can see the first sunrise of the year to wish for your luck. At this festival, you can also enjoy diverse performances that celebrate New Year's Day. (December 31st and January 1st)

Daegwallyeong Snow Festival
대관령 눈꽃 축제 deh-gwahl-lyuhng noon-ggot chook-jjeh

Daegwallyeong is the place in Korea where it snows the most. For about 10 days every year in January, huge snow and ice sculptures are on display, and you can also ride the snowmobile train. (Mid January)

Film festivals
영화제 yuhng-hwah-jeh

Busan International Film Festival

부산 국제 영화제 boo-sahn gook-jjeh yuhng-hwah-jeh

The most famous and biggest international film festival in Asia. (Early October)

Jeonju International Film Festival

전주 국제 영화제 jawn-joo gook-jjeh yuhng-hwah-jeh

This festival is smaller than the BIFF, but you can enjoy the sights in historic Jeonju in addition to the festival. (Early May)

Bucheon International Fantastic Film Festival

부천 국제 판타스틱 영화제
boo-chawn gook-jjeh pahn-tah-seu-teek yuhng-hwah-jeh

This film festival focuses on horror, thriller, mystery, and fantasy films. (Mid ~ Late July)

Music festivals
음악 축제 eu-mahk chook-jjeh

Jarasum International Jazz Festival

자라섬 국제 재즈 페스티벌

jah-rah-sawm gook-jjeh jjeh-jeu peh-seu-tee-bawl

The most famous jazz festival in Korea, where dozens of international jazz artists perform. Over 100,000 people visit this festival every year. (Mid October)

Incheon Pentaport Rock Festival

인천 펜타포트 락 페스티벌

een-chawn pehn-tah-po-teu rahk peh-seu-tee-bawl

One of the biggest live music events in Korea. The festival mainly features rock and electronic music. (Mid August)

Seoul Jazz Festival

서울 재즈 페스티벌 saw-wool jjeh-jeu peh-seu-tee-bawl

The second biggest Jazz festival in Korea with a lineup of big-name musicians from Korea and abroad. (Late May)

BUSY AREAS IN SEOUL

Where is the nearest subway station?

여기서 제일 가까운 지하철 역이 어디예요?

Yuh-gee-saw jay-eel gah-ggah-woon jee-hah-chawl
yuh-gee aw-dee-yeh-yo?

Track 38

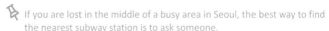

If you are lost in the middle of a busy area in Seoul, the best way to find
the nearest subway station is to ask someone.

Hongdae

홍대 hong-deh

An extremely popular area among younger people surrounding Hongik
University. This area used to be a place for poor artists and Indie musicians to
gather. Since the main area has become very commercialized with cafes and
shops, the artists and musicians moved toward the outskirts of Hongdae to
areas such as Yeonnam-dong.

Sinchon/Edae

신촌/이대 sheen-chon/ee-deh

Two of the most prestigious universities are in this area: Yonsei University and Ewha Womans University. Due to this, there are many affordable clothing and accessory stores as well as very reasonably priced restaurants.

Myeongdong

명동 myuhng-dong

Myeongdong has almost everything a shopper could ever want available in one area. From the main branches of the top Korean department stores, Lotte and Shinsegae, to H&M and more Korean cosmetics shops than you can count, this neighborhood is a shopping mecca for Koreans and tourists alike. Fashion and shopping aside, Myeongdong is home to one of the most prominent Catholic cathedrals in Korea. The official name of the church is The Cathedral Church of the Virgin Mary of the Immaculate Conception, but it is also known as just simply Myeongdong Cathedral.

Jongno

종로 jong-no

Seoul's modern "downtown" mixed with "old town" flair. Among the government office buildings, gigantic bookstores, and bars and restaurants, you will find many historical sites, gardens, old movie theaters, and traditional street markets.

Insadong

인사동 een-sah-dong

A popular neighborhood in Jongno, the heart of Seoul, where there are many opportunities to experience traditional Korean culture. Visit traditional teahouses and restaurants, craft workshops (traditional Korean knot-tying, making kimchi, ceramic painting, etc.), antique shops, art galleries, souvenir stores, and more!

Samcheongdong

삼청동 sahm-chawng-dong

Offers some of the best scenery in Seoul. Gyeongbok Palace and the Blue
House (home of the President of Korea) are located here, and the area is well-
known for its many traditional 한옥 [hah-nok] (Korean-style homes). Many
quirky shops, art galleries, and upscale restaurants have popped up in this area
in recent years, which gives the area a unique and trendy vibe.

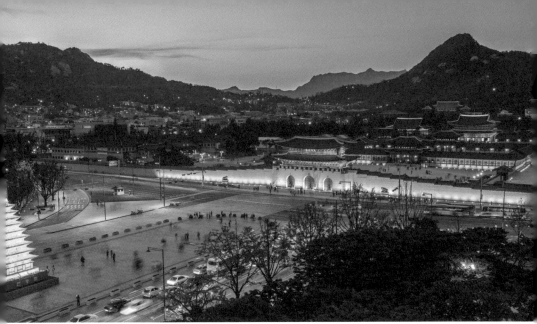

Gwanghwamun Square

광화문 광장 gwahng-hwah-moon gwahng-jahng

Opened in 2009, Gwanghwamun Square is located just in front of the entrance of Gyeongbok Palace. A statue of Admiral Yi and the 12.23 Fountain stand guard while a statue of King Sejong the Great sits atop an underground museum (the stairs to The Story of King Sejong Exhibition Hall, which is connected to the Admiral Yi Museum, are located at the backside of the King Sejong statue). This location became quite the social gathering spot for large-scale events such as Pope Francis's visit, candlelight vigils, and a watch party for the Korean national soccer team during the World Cup. Gwanghwamun Square is in the middle of a busy 10-lane major roadway, so be sure to use one of the three crosswalks to get there!

Yeouido

여의도 yuh-ee-do

The business and financial center of Korea, also known for the National Assembly of the Republic of Korea, numerous broadcasting stations, the 63 building, and IFC Mall. On weekends, people often visit Yeouido Park or Yeouido Han River Park.

Gangnam Station

강남역 gahng-nahm-nyuhk

An incredibly busy and affluent area densely packed with shops, restaurants, cafes, pubs, clubs, office buildings, and many private English institutes and "cram schools".

Apgujeong/Cheongdam/Sinsa

압구정/청담/신사 ahp-ggoo-jawng/chawng-dahm/sheen-sah

The swankiest areas in Seoul. There are many upscale boutiques, makeup studios, wedding dress shops, and entertainment companies in this neighborhood. In Apgujeong resides a not-so-typical tourist information center; the Gangnam Tourist Information Center has two levels where you can exchange currency, store your luggage, get information on the area and for medical tourism, and experience Korean popular music and TV soap opera culture (known as Hallyu, or 한류 [hahl-lyou]).

Daehangno

대학로 deh-hahng-no

Many theaters are located in this area, especially small theaters for plays. Since Sungkyunkwan University is nearby, and Seoul National University used to be located in this area, you can experience a youthful and romantic ambiance while walking around.

Itaewon

이태원 ee-teh-won

A unique neighborhood abound with multiculturalism that is also located within walking distance of United States Army Garrison Yongsan. The large and growing international community in Itaewon has really helped in building up the area and popularizing it with tourists and locals. Whether it is food, shopping, or nightlife, Itaewon has it all. It has become somewhat of a foodie destination in recent years, as it is here you can find nearly any cuisine your heart desires, from vegan (visit PLANT) and southern United States barbecue (Linus BBQ is a crowd favorite), to a large number of halal restaurants and Korean-Mexican fusion (visit Coreanos or Vatos Tacos). Additionally, if you are looking to buy larger shoes or clothing, there are a large number of "Big and Tall" or "Big Size" shops in Itaewon.

Dongdaemun/Namdaemun
동대문/남대문 dong-deh-moon/nahm-deh-moon

Dongdaemun literally translates to "big east door", and Namdaemun translates to "big south door". Although both locations are gates which were built during the Joseon Dynasty, today these areas are more well-known for the very large traditional markets which have any and every type of shop imaginable.

Big shopping complexes/multicultural facilities in Seoul

Dongdaemun Design Plaza
동대문 DDP
dong-deh-moon dee-dee-pee

IFC Mall in Yeouido
여의도 IFC몰
yuh-ee-do ah-ee-eh-peu-ssee-mol

D-Cube City in Sindorim
신도림 디큐브시티
sheen-do-reem dee-kyou-beu-ssee-tee

COEX Mall in Samseongdong
삼성역 COEX몰
sahm-sawng-yuhk ko-ehk-sseu-mol

Yeongdeungpo Times Square
영등포 타임스퀘어
yuhng-deung-po tah-eem-seu-kweh-aw

Han River

한강 hahn-gahng

The Han River runs through the middle of Seoul and served as a valuable transportation route in the past. Nowadays, the river is lined with many parks and bicycle and jogging paths. Many Seoulites take advantage of the parks when the weather is nice to have picnics on the weekends, or use the paths to walk, jog, or cycle along the river. There is even a set of three man-made floating islands on the river where you have the opportunity to shop, eat, or attend a public event.

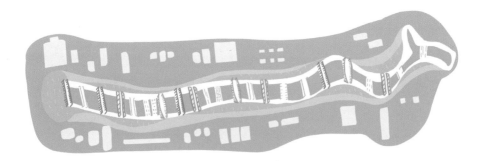

Cheonggyecheon Stream

청계천 chawng-gyeh-chawn

A modern stream that starts at Cheonggye Plaza (look for Spring Tower, the tall, multi-colored conch art piece, and Candelight Fountain, a double-layer waterfall) and runs through the Jung District (중구 [joong-goo]) and Jongno District (종로구 [jong-no-goo]) before emptying into the Han River. Along the stream are pedestrian walkways and places to dip your feet to cool off on those hot and humid Korean summer days.

VISITING
A LOCAL CITY

강원도

안동시

전주한옥마을

경주시

담양군
죽녹원

통영시

부산시

순천시
순천만

여수시
오동도

남해군

외도

제주도

Gangwon Province

강원도 gahng-won-do

Korea's most northeasterly and most rural province. It is here where you can enjoy beautiful parks, mountains, rivers, and beaches. It is a favorite spot for short trips from Seoul. There are many Korean-style rental cottages and facilities for outdoor activities.

Busan City

부산시 boo-sahn-shee

The second largest city in Korea. A port city, Busan has something for everyone: incredibly fresh seafood, sunny beaches with picturesque views, mountains for hiking, chic cafes, and the world's largest department store, Shinsegae Centum City. A few popular Korean movies and dramas were set in Busan in recent years which has boosted tourism from both international tourists and Koreans.

Gyeongju City

경주시 gyuhng-joo-shee

As the capital city during the Silla Kingdom for almost 1,000 years, Gyeongju is an incredibly important historical city. Most Korean people have been here at least once on a school field trip at some point. It is here where a vast number of archaeological sites and cultural artifacts from the Silla Kingdom remain.

Andong City

안동시 ahn-dong-shee

The most "Korean" city in all of Korea. Buildings, items, and certain aspects of ancient Korean culture from the Joseon Dynasty have been preserved here. The Hahoe Folk Village has 120 houses which are 300-500 years old, and is the most famous and one of the most frequented villages.

Namhae County

남해군 nah-meh-goon

Consists of 68 picturesque little islands. Most of the people live on the two biggest islands, Namhaedo and Changseondo. The southernmost part of Namhaedo is part of Hallyeohaesang National Marine Park, which was designated a national park in 1968.

Tongyeong City & Geoje island

통영시 tong-yuhng-shee 거제도 gaw-jeh-do

Tongyeong City is part of Hallyeohaesang National Marine Park, and there are many historical sites dedicated or related to the great Admiral Yi Sunsin. Geoje Island is the second biggest island after Jeju Island in Korea, and it is connected to Tongyeong City.

Oe Island

와도 weh-do

A private island that is also part of Hallyeohaesang National Marine Park and is located 4km away from Geoje island. You cannot spend the night on the island, so people visit during the day for the huge botanical garden.

Suncheon Bay in Suncheon City

순천시 순천만 soon-chawn-shee soon-chawn-mahn

An enormous field of reeds on the beach. If you visit in the summer, the reed beds are vibrant green, but they fade during autumn and into winter. Suncheon Bay is designated as a nature preservation district, giving visitors the opportunity to view some of the 200 plus types of birds, including 11 rare species.

Hanok Village in Jeonju City

전주시 한옥마을 jawn-joo-shee hah-nok-mah-eul

Designated as a Korean-style house (Hanok) preservation district with over 700 houses, some of which are still home to residents today. After it became a special tourist zone, however, many residents left the village, and more retail shops and restaurants have opened up.

Odong Island in Yeosu City

여수시 오동도 yuh-soo-shee o-dong-do

An tiny island which belongs to Hallyeohaesang National Marine Park. There were many "Odong" trees (Paulownia trees) on the island at one point, which is how it got its name. Currently, instead of Odong trees, there are nearly 200 rare species of other types of trees.

Bamboo Forest in Damyang County

담양군 죽녹원 dah-myahng-goon joong-no-gwon

160,000 square meters of bamboo to walk through and help alleviate stress. Not only can you enjoy strolling through the bamboo forest, but there is a chance to eat daetong-bap (rice steamed in a bamboo container) and tteokgalbi (minced, seasoned, and grilled beef rib meat). The incredibly famous "Metasequoia Road" is also here.

Jeju Island

제주도 jeh-joo-do

With its warm climate, white sand beaches, a dormant volcano, natural waterfalls, and the Olle Walking Trails, Jeju Island has become the most popular holiday spot in Korea among international and domestic travelers.

Cultural tip: In Korea, you might come across some restrooms where you need to squat down, especially in old buildings or subway stations. At some rest stops on the highway, look at the signs on the door to see whether or not the toilet inside is western-style or squat.

1. At a bus terminal

Track 40

One adult ticket and one children's ticket for <u>Gwangju</u>, please.

<u>광주</u> 어른 한 장, 어린이 한 장이요.

<u>Gwahng-joo</u> aw-reun hahn jahng, aw-ree-nee hahn jahng-ee-yo.

You can replace Gwangju with your destination.

Paper/Ticket : 장

1 ticket	한 장	hahn jahng	6 tickets	여섯 장	yuh-sawt jjahng
2 tickets	두 장	doo jahng	7 tickets	일곱 장	eel-gop jjahng
3 tickets	세 장	seh jahng	8 tickets	여덟 장	yuh-dawl jjahng
4 tickets	네 장	neh jahng	9 tickets	아홉 장	ah-hop jjahng
5 tickets	다섯 장	dah-sawt jjahng	10 tickets	열 장	yuhl jjahng

2. At a train station

Track 41

Related phrases:

Does this train go to <u>Andong</u>?

안동 가는 기차 맞아요?

<u>Ahn-dong</u> gah-neun gee-chah mah-jah-yo?

Where do I take the train bound for <u>Andong</u>?

안동 가는 기차 어디서 타는 거예요?

<u>Ahn-dong</u> gah-neun gee-chah aw-dee-saw tah-neun gaw-yeh-yo?

 You can replace Andong with your destination.

EMERGENCIES

Related phrases:

Excuse me.
저기요.
Jaw-gee-yo.

Please help me.
도와주세요.
Do-wah-joo-seh-yo.

Please call 119.
119 좀 불러 주세요.
Eel-leel-goo jom bool-law joo-seh-yo.

I don't speak Korean.
저는 한국말 못 해요.
Jaw-neun hahn-goong-mahl mo teh-yo.

1. At a hospital/pharmacy

Where does it hurt?
어디가 아파요?

My stomach hurts.
배 아파요.

Aw-dee-gah ah-pah-yo?

<u>Beh</u> ah-pah-yo.

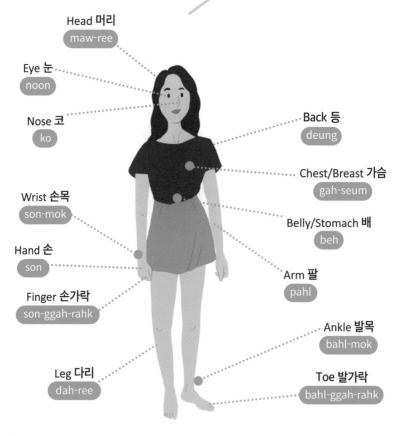

I hurt my leg.

다리 다쳤어요.

Dah-ree dah-chyuh-ssaw-yo.

Other possibilities:

Head 머리
maw-ree

Eye 눈
noon

Nose 코
ko

Back 등
deung

Chest/Breast 가슴
gah-seum

Wrist 손목
son-mok

Belly/Stomach 배
beh

Hand 손
son

Arm 팔
pahl

Finger 손가락
son-ggah-rahk

Ankle 발목
bahl-mok

Leg 다리
dah-ree

Toe 발가락
bahl-ggah-rahk

Please refer to page 136 for more body part terms.

Related phrase:

Multi-symptom cold/flu medicine, please.

종합 감기약 주세요.

Jong-hahp gahm-gee-yahk joo-seh-yo.

Other possibilities:

Cough medicine
기침약
gee-cheem-nyahk

Sinus cold medicine
코감기 약
ko-gahm-gee yahk

Sore throat medicine
목감기 약
mok-ggahm-gee yahk

Headache medicine
두통약
doo-tong-nyahk

Diarrhea medicine
설사약
sawl-ssah-yahk

Motion sickness medicine
멀미약
mawl-mee-yahk

2. At a lost & found or police office

My camera was stolen.
카메라 도둑 맞았어요.

Please fill out this form.
여기 서류 작성해 주세요.

Kah-meh-rah do-dook mah-jah-ssaw-yo.

Yuh-gee saw-ryou jahk-ssawng-heh joo-seh-yo.

Related phrases:

I've lost my bag.

가방 잃어버렸어요.

Gah-bahng ee-raw-baw-ryuh-ssaw-yo.

I left my cell phone (on the subway/bus/taxi).

핸드폰을 놓고 내렸어요.

hehn-deu-pon-eul no-ko neh-ryuh-ssaw-yo.

Other possibilities:

wallet
지갑

jee-gahp

money
돈

don

passport
여권

yuh-ggwon

sunglasses
선글라스

ssawn-geul-lah-sseu

MORE ABOUT
KOREAN LANGUAGE

1. Quick guide to 한글 (Hangeul)

The Korean writing system, Hangeul, is the only writing system in the world in which the name of its creator and founding date are known. King Sejong the Great, who was the fourth king of the Joseon Dynasty, developed Hangeul in the 15th century with the help of scholars from the royal research institute, Jiphyeonjeon. King Sejong despised using Hanja, or Chinese characters, to write in Korean, so he developed a system so that all people could read and write, not just those in higher social classes.

Hangeul, therefore, was invented for anyone to logically understand and easily learn by heart, without much effort to memorize. Some people say that it takes one day or even one hour for non-native speakers to master reading Hangeul. It is highly recommended you take some time to study Hangeul letters because once you have mastered it, you will be able to read any Korean word. So, let's get started!

In Hangeul, there are 24 basic letters and digraphs.
*digraph: pair of characters used to make one sound (phoneme)

Of the letters, 14 are consonants (자음) and five of them are doubled to form five tense consonants (쌍자음).

Consonants

Basic	ㄱ	ㄴ	ㄷ	ㄹ	ㅁ	ㅂ	ㅅ	ㅇ	ㅈ	ㅊ	ㅋ	ㅌ	ㅍ	ㅎ
	g/k	n	d/t	r/l	m	b/p	s	ng	j	ch	k	t	p	h
	g/k	n	d/t	r/l	m	b/p	s/ɕ	ŋ	dʑ/tɕ	tɕʰ	k/kʰ	t/tʰ	p/pʰ	h

Tense	ㄲ		ㄸ			ㅃ	ㅆ		ㅉ					
	kk		tt			pp	ss		jj					
	k'		t'			p'	s'		c'					

When it comes to vowels (모음), there are 10 basic letters. 11 additional letters can be created by combining certain basic letters to make a total of 21 vowels. Of the vowels, eight are single pure vowels, also known as monophthongs (단모음), and 13 are diphthongs (이중모음), or two vowel sounds joined into one syllable which creates one sound.

* When saying a monophthong, you are producing one pure vowel with no tongue movement.

* When saying a diphthong, you are producing one sound by saying two vowels. Therefore, your tongue and mouth move quickly from one letter to another (glide or slide) to create a single sound.

Vowels

Monophthongs	ㅏ	ㅓ	ㅗ	ㅜ	ㅡ	ㅣ	ㅐ	ㅔ
	a	eo	o	u	eu	i	ae	e
	a/aː	ʌ/əː	o/oː	u/uː	ɨ/ɯː	i/iː	ɛ/ɛː	e/eː

Diphthongs	ㅑ	ㅕ	ㅛ	ㅠ		ㅒ	ㅖ
	ya	yeo	yo	yu		yae	ye
	ja	jʌ	jo	ju		jɛ	je
	ㅘ	ㅝ				ㅙ	ㅞ
	wa	wo				wae	we
	wa	wʌ/wəː				wɛ	we
					ㅚ	ㅟ	ㅢ
					oe	wi	ui
					we	wi	ɨi

* ㅚ and ㅟ were pronounced as single pure vowels (monophthongs) in the past; however, presently, these vowels are produced as two vowels gradually gliding into one another to create one sound (diphthong).

Writing 한글 letters

한글 is written top to bottom, left to right. For example:

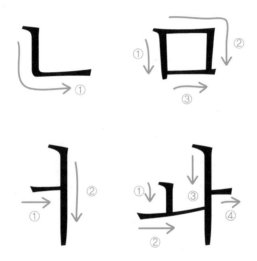

By making sure you follow the stroke order rules, you will find that writing Korean is quite easy and other people will be able to better read your handwriting.

Syllable blocks

Each Korean syllable is written in a way that forms a block-like shape, with each letter inside the block forming a sound/syllable.

ㅊ + ㅣ + ㄴ (ch+i+n) = chin
ㄱ + ㅜ (g+u) = gu
친 (chin) + 구 (gu) = 친구 (chingu) = "friend"

In each syllable block, there is a:

1. *Beginning consonant
2. *Middle vowel
3. Optional final consonant

*Required in a syllable block. A block MUST contain a minimum of two letters: 1 consonant and 1 vowel.

Two of the most common ways to write consonant and vowel combinations in Korean are horizontally and vertically (the boxes drawn here are for illustrative purpose only).

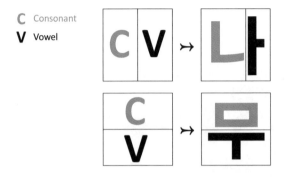

By adding a final consonant (받침), the blocks are modified:

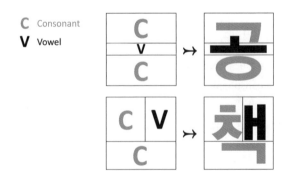

There are also syllables which have two final consonants, such as:

*In all the syllable blocks, the letters are either compressed or stretched to keep the size relatively the same as the other letters.

Vowels

Since the "minimum two letter" rule exists and one letter has to be a consonant and the other has to be a vowel, what can you do when a vowel needs to be written in its own syllable block? Add the consonant ○ [ng] in front of or on top of the vowel. When reading a vowel, such as 아, the ○ makes no sound and you just pronounce the ㅏ [a].

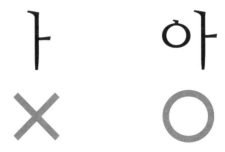

*Vowels absolutely, cannot, under any circumstances be written by themselves!!

2. Numbers

0	영 / 공	yuhng / gong
1	일	eel
2	이	ee
3	삼	sahm
4	사	sah
5	오	o
6	육	youk
7	칠	cheel
8	팔	pahl
9	구	goo
10	십	sheep
11	십일	shee-beel
12	십이	shee-bee
13	십삼	sheep-sahm
14	십사	sheep-sah
15	십오	shee-bo
16	십육	sheem-nyouk
17	십칠	sheep-cheel
18	십팔	sheep-pahl
19	십구	sheep-goo
20	이십	ee-sheep
21	이십일	ee-shee-beel
22	이십이	ee-shee-bee
23	이십삼	ee-sheep-sahm
24	이십사	ee-sheep-sah
25	이십오	ee-shee-bo

26	이십육	ee-sheem-nyouk
27	이십칠	ee-sheep-cheel
28	이십팔	ee-sheep-pahl
29	이십구	ee-sheep-goo
30	삼십	sahm-sheep
31	삼십일	sahm-shee-beel
32	삽십이	sahm-shee-bee
33	삼십삼	sahm-sheep-sahm
34	삼십사	sahm-sheep-sah
35	삼십오	sahm-shee-bo
36	삼십육	sahm-sheem-nyouk
37	삼십칠	sahm-sheep-cheel
38	삼십팔	sahm-sheep-pahl
39	삼십구	sahm-sheep-goo
40	사십	sah-sheep
41	사십일	sah-shee-beel
42	사십이	sah-shee-bee
43	사십삼	sah-sheep-sahm
44	사십사	sah-sheep-sah
45	사십오	sah-shee-bo
46	사십육	sah-sheem-nyouk
47	사십칠	sah-sheep-cheel
48	사십팔	sah-sheep-pahl
49	사십구	sah-sheep-goo
50	오십	o-sheep

51	오십일	o-shee-beel	77	칠십칠	cheel-sheep-cheel
52	오십이	o-shee-bee	78	칠십팔	cheel-sheep-pahl
53	오십삼	o-sheep-sahm	79	칠십구	cheel-sheep-goo
54	오십사	o-sheep-sah	80	팔십	pahl-sheep
55	오십오	o-shee-bo	81	팔십일	pahl-shee-beel
56	오십육	o-sheem-nyouk	82	팔십이	pahl-shee-bee
57	오십칠	o-sheep-cheel	83	팔십삼	pahl-sheep-sahm
58	오십팔	o-sheep-pahl	84	팔십사	pahl-sheep-sah
59	오십구	o-sheep-goo	85	팔십오	pahl-shee-bo
60	육십	youk-sheep	86	팔십육	pahl-sheem-nyouk
61	육십일	youk-shee-beel	87	팔십칠	pahl-sheep-cheel
62	육십이	youk-shee-bee	88	팔십팔	pahl-sheep-pahl
63	육십삼	youk-sheep-sahm	89	팔십구	pahl-sheep-goo
64	육십사	youk-sheep-sah	90	구십	goo-sheep
65	육십오	youk-shee-bo	91	구십일	goo-shee-beel
66	육십육	youk-sheem-nyouk	92	구십이	goo-shee-bee
67	육십칠	youk-sheep-cheel	93	구십삼	goo-sheep-sahm
68	육십팔	youk-sheep-pahl	94	구십사	goo-sheep-sah
69	육십구	youk-sheep-goo	95	구십오	goo-shee-bo
70	칠십	cheel-sheep	96	구십육	goo-sheem-nyouk
71	칠십일	cheel-shee-beel	97	구십칠	goo-sheep-cheel
72	칠십이	cheel-shee-bee	98	구십팔	goo-sheep-pahl
73	칠십삼	cheel-sheep-sahm	99	구십구	goo-sheep-goo
74	칠십사	cheel-sheep-sah	100	백	behk
75	칠십오	cheel-shee-bo	1000	천	chawn
76	칠십육	cheel-sheem-nyouk			

If you know how to count up to 10, you can combine the numbers to form bigger numbers, starting with 11.

12 = 10 + 2 = 십 + 이
= 십이 shee-bee

333 = 3 x 100 + 3 x 10 + 3 = 삼 x 백 + 삼 x 십 + 삼
= 삼백삼십삼 sahm-behk-sahm-sheep-sahm

4977 = 4 x 1000 + 9 x 100 + 7 x 10 + 7 = 사 x 천 + 구 x 백 + 칠 x 십 + 칠
= 사천구백칠십칠 sah-chawn-goo-behk-cheel-sheep-cheel

Months

January	1월	ee-rwol	July	7월	chee-rwol
February	2월	ee-wol	August	8월	pah-rwol
March	3월	sah-mwol	September	9월	goo-wol
April	4월	sah-wol	October	10월	shee-wol
May	5월	o-wol	November	11월	shee-bee-rwol
June	6월	you-wol	December	12월	shee-bee-wol

Days

1st (day of the month)	1일	ee-reel	17th (day of the month)	17일	sheep-chee-reel
2nd (day of the month)	2일	ee-eel	18th (day of the month)	18일	sheep-pah-reel
3rd (day of the month)	3일	sah-meel	19th (day of the month)	19일	sheep-goo-eel
4th (day of the month)	4일	sah-eel	20th (day of the month)	20일	ee-shee-beel
5th (day of the month)	5일	o-eel	21st (day of the month)	21일	ee-shee-bee-reel
6th (day of the month)	6일	you-geel	22nd (day of the month)	22일	ee-shee-bee-eel
7th (day of the month)	7일	chee-reel	23rd (day of the month)	23일	ee-sheep-sah-meel
8th (day of the month)	8일	pah-reel	24th (day of the month)	24일	ee-sheep-sah-eel
9th (day of the month)	9일	goo-eel	25th (day of the month)	25일	ee-shee-bo-eel
10th (day of the month)	10일	shee-beel	26th (day of the month)	26일	ee-sheem-nyou-geel
11th (day of the month)	11일	shee-bee-reel	27th (day of the month)	27일	ee-sheep-chee-reel
12th (day of the month)	12일	shee-bee-eel	28th (day of the month)	28일	ee-sheep-pah-reel
13th (day of the month)	13일	sheep-sah-meel	29th (day of the month)	29일	ee-sheep-goo-eel
14th (day of the month)	14일	sheep-sah-eel	30th (day of the month)	30일	sahm-shee-beel
15th (day of the month)	15일	shee-bo-eel	31st (day of the month)	31일	sahm-shee-bee-reel
16th (day of the month)	16일	sheem-nyou-geel			

Hours

1 o'clock	**한 시**	hahn shee
2 o'clock	**두 시**	doo shee
3 o'clock	**세 시**	seh shee
4 o'clock	**네 시**	neh shee
5 o'clock	**다섯 시**	dah-sawt shee
6 o'clock	**여섯 시**	yuh-sawt shee
7 o'clock	**일곱 시**	eel-gop shee
8 o'clock	**여덟 시**	yuh-dawl shee
9 o'clock	**아홉 시**	ah-hop shee
10 o'clock	**열 시**	yuhl shee
11 o'clock	**열한 시**	yuh-rahn shee
12 o'clock	**열두 시**	yuhl-doo shee

Minutes

1 minute	일 분	eel boon	16 minutes	십육 분	sheem-nyouk bboon
2 minutes	이 분	ee boon	17 minutes	십칠 분	sheep-cheel boon
3 minutes	삼 분	sahm boon	18 minutes	십팔 분	sheep-pahl boon
4 minutes	사 분	sah boon	19 minutes	십구 분	sheep-goo boon
5 minutes	오 분	o boon	20 minutes	이십 분	ee-sheep bboon
6 minutes	육 분	youk bboon	21 minutes	이십일 분	ee-shee-beel boon
7 minutes	칠 분	cheel boon	22 minutes	이십이 분	ee-shee-bee boon
8 minutes	팔 분	pahl boon	23 minutes	이십삼 분	ee-sheep-sahm boon
9 minutes	구 분	goo boon	24 minutes	이십사 분	ee-sheep-sah boon
10 minutes	십 분	sheep bboon	25 minutes	이십오 분	ee-shee-bo boon
11 minutes	십일 분	shee-beel boon	26 minutes	이십육 분	ee-sheem-nyouk boon
12 minutes	십이 분	shee-bee boon	27 minutes	이십칠 분	ee-sheep-cheel boon
13 minutes	십삼 분	sheep-sahm boon	28 minutes	이십팔 분	ee-sheep-pahl boon
14 minutes	십사 분	sheep-sah boon	29 minutes	이십구 분	ee-sheep-goo boon
15 minutes	십오 분	shee-bo boon	30 minutes	삼십 분	sahm-sheep bboon

31 minutes	삼십일 분	sahm-shee-beel boon	46 minutes	사십육 분	sah-sheem-nyouk boon
32 minutes	삼십이 분	sahm-shee-bee boon	47 minutes	사십칠 분	sah-sheep-cheel boon
33 minutes	삼십삼 분	sahm-sheep-sahm boon	48 minutes	사십팔 분	sah-sheep-pahl boon
34 minutes	삼십사 분	sahm-sheep-sah boon	49 minutes	사십구 분	sah-sheep-goo boon
35 minutes	삼십오 분	sahm-shee-bo boon	50 minutes	오십 분	o-sheep bboon
36 minutes	삼십육 분	sahm-sheem-nyouk boon	51 minutes	오십일 분	o-shee-beel boon
37 minutes	삼십칠 분	sahm-sheep-cheel boon	52 minutes	오십이 분	o-shee-bee boon
38 minutes	삼십팔 분	sahm-sheep-pahl boon	53 minutes	오십삼 분	o-sheep-sahm boon
39 minutes	삼십구 분	sahm-sheep-goo boon	54 minutes	오십사 분	o-sheep-sah boon
40 minutes	사십 분	sah-sheep bboon	55 minutes	오십오 분	o-shee-bo boon
41 minutes	사십일 분	sah-shee-beel boon	56 minutes	오십육 분	o-sheem-nyouk boon
42 minutes	사십이 분	sah-shee-bee boon	57 minutes	오십칠 분	o-sheep-cheel boon
43 minutes	사십삼 분	sah-sheep-sahm boon	58 minutes	오십팔 분	o-sheep-pahl boon
44 minutes	사십사 분	sah-sheep-sah boon	59 minutes	오십구 분	o-sheep-goo boon
45 minutes	사십오 분	sah-shee-bo boon	60 minutes	육십 분	youk-sheep bboon

Building floor numbers

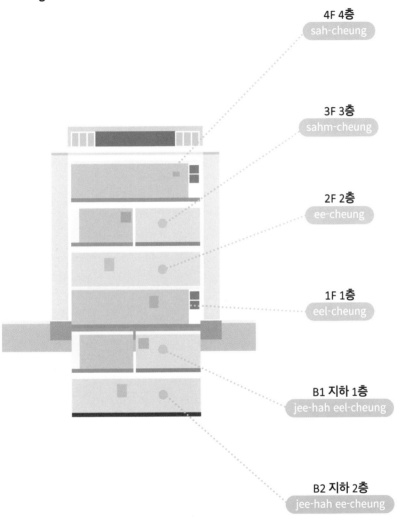

4F 4층
sah-cheung

3F 3층
sahm-cheung

2F 2층
ee-cheung

1F 1층
eel-cheung

B1 지하 1층
jee-hah eel-cheung

B2 지하 2층
jee-hah ee-cheung

Counters

Objects: 개

1 item	한 개	hahn geh	6 items	여섯 개	yuh-sawt ggeh
2 items	두 개	doo geh	7 items	일곱 개	eel-gop ggeh
3 items	세 개	seh geh	8 items	여덟 개	yuh-dawl ggeh
4 items	네 개	neh geh	9 items	아홉 개	ah-hop ggeh
5 items	다섯 개	dah-sawt ggeh	10 items	열 개	yul ggeh

People: 명

1 person	한 명	hahn myuhng	6 people	여섯 명	yuh-sawn myuhng
2 people	두 명	doo myuhng	7 people	일곱 명	eel-gom myuhng
3 people	세 명	seh myuhng	8 people	여덟 명	yuh-dawl myuhng
4 people	네 명	neh myuhng	9 people	아홉 명	ah-hom myuhng
5 people	다섯 명	dah-sawn myuhng	10 people	열 명	yul myuhng

Food servings: 인분

One serving	1인분	ee-reen-boon	Six servings	6인분	you-geen-boon
Two servings	2인분	ee-een-boon	Seven servings	7인분	chee-reen-boon
Three servings	3인분	sa-meen-boon	Eight servings	8인분	pah-reen-boon
Four servings	4인분	sah-een-boon	Nine servings	9인분	goo-een-boon
Five servings	5인분	o-een-boon	Ten servings	10인분	shee-been-boon

Papers/Tickets : 장

1 ticket	한 장	hahn jahng	6 tickets	여섯 장	yuh-sawt jjahng
2 tickets	두 장	doo jahng	7 tickets	일곱 장	eel-gop jjahng
3 tickets	세 장	seh jahng	8 tickets	여덟 장	yuh-dawl jjahng
4 tickets	네 장	neh jahng	9 tickets	아홉 장	ah-hop jjahng
5 tickets	다섯 장	dah-sawt jjahng	10 tickets	열 장	yul jjahng

Korean Money 원

Coins

10원 / 십 원	**50원 / 오십 원**	**100원 / 백 원**	**500원 / 오백 원**
sheeb won	o-sheeb won	beg won	o-beg won

Bills

1,000원 / 천 원	**5,000원 / 오천 원**
chawn won	o-chawn won

10,000원 / 만 원	**50,000원 / 오만 원**
mahn won	o-mahn won

3. Directions

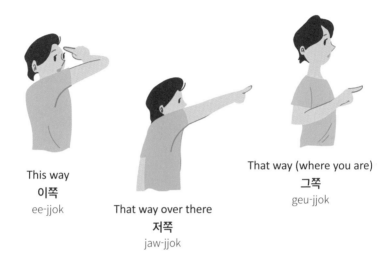

This way
이쪽
ee-jjok

That way over there
저쪽
jaw-jjok

That way (where you are)
그쪽
geu-jjok

Left
왼쪽
wehn-jjok

Right
오른쪽
o-reun-jjok

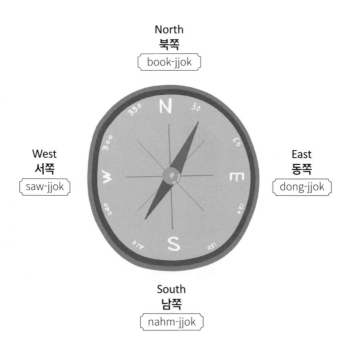

North
북쪽
book-jjok

West
서쪽
saw-jjok

East
동쪽
dong-jjok

South
남쪽
nahm-jjok

Left turn
좌회전
jwah-hweh-jawn

Go straight
직진
jeek-jjeen

Right turn
우회전
woo-hweh-jawn

LEARN MORE EFFECTIVELY
WITH OUR PREMIUM COURSES

My Virtual Korean Friends: Korean Speaking Practice

▶ 🖾 8

My Virtual Korean Friends: Korean Speaking Practice

▶ 🖾 11

My First Korean Phrases (Explained in Korean)

🎧 🖾 20

My Virtual Korean Friends: Korean Speaking Practice

▶ 🖾 10

Listen & Repeat: The Korean Verbs Guide

🎧 🖾 10

Korean Folk Tales: Short & interesting stories for learners

🎧 🖾 20

Gain unlimited access to hundreds of video and audio lessons by becoming a Premium Member at our website, **https://talktomeinkorean.com**! Practice your pronunciation and further improve your listening skills through our online courses.

Courses available online include our Korean Pronunciation Guide course, which is directly related to this book, Korean Dictation Test course, Listen & Repeat course, and more.

TTMIK Book Audio App

Download our app **TTMIK: Audio** to listen to all the audio and video tracks from our book conveniently on your phone! The app is available for free on both iOS and Android. Search for **TTMIK: Audio** in your app store.